MONUMENTAL SILVER LININGS

MONUMENTAL SILVER LININGS
ONE SEXUAL ASSAULT SURVIVOR'S QUEST FOR JUSTICE

MACKENZIE SEVERNS

ISBN 978-1-7353289-0-4

Cover designed by Kazi Zubair

Edited by Ella Medler

With the exception of any characters addressed by
their first and last name, all the characters names have
been changed and identifying details have been al-
tered. Characters addressed by their first and last name
have given the author explicit permission to use their
names, except for my rapist who does not deserve such
courtesy. His name is Vicente Pastor.

FOR MY PARENTS, WHO ARE MY
GREATEST SUPPORTERS

Contents

INTRODUCTION

The issue with introductions is that I never know what to write. Whether I am crafting an introduction to an English essay, or toiling away trying to write this intro, I struggle. I am not an established author, at least not yet; furthermore, I have no idea where to begin.

I guess that means I will have to start at the beginning.

There are some considerations that I want anyone who reads this to keep in mind. When addressing various people in my life, I address them by nicknames, or I have changed their names completely. If someone has given me explicit permission to include their name, I use their first and last name.

The second paramount factor is that I write when

I am upset. I find journaling to be a way to release anger and frustration; therefore, I tend to comment more about the bad aspects of relationships in my life rather than the good ones. One prime example of this is my depiction of my mother. I love her to death, and I appreciate everything that she has done to hold my family together, but I have a tendency to write about her when I am upset with her. In reality, my mom kept me sane. She is the most vital part of my support system. Her strength is astounding.

I was drugged and raped when I was fifteen, on an exchange in Lima, Peru. This compilation of journal entries depicts my life shortly before the rape and how the rape impacted me and those around me. I am telling my story not only to help spread awareness about sexual assault, but also to let sexual assault survivors who read my story know that they are not alone. I want to be a voice for sexual assault survivors who can't speak up. I was fortunate that my circumstances enabled me to tell my story. Throughout my journey, I have met many survivors, and each one has their unique story. I appreciate everyone who has shared their difficult stories with me. I hope that my story motivates others to speak out. Sexual assault is not something that should be dealt with in silence. Throughout the entries, at various times, I stress that I regret telling my parents about what happened to me, but looking back, telling my parents is by far the best decision I've ever made.

JUNE

Los Angeles: Thursday, June 14th, 2018
I wake up relatively well rested and walk outside to my front patio to drink coffee with my mom. I'm sad because this is the last day I have to spend with her before leaving for Peru.

Afterwards, I drive to the beach to hang out with my boyfriend, Elliott. We talk about our plans for approaching the summer. This summer I'm traveling to Peru, and Elliott is traveling to Paris.

Last week, I told Elliott that I thought we should take a break over the summer. I could tell that he was hurt by that conversation. I want to live my life to the fullest. I'm only fifteen, which is way too young to have a three-month long-distance relationship. We lie down to relax on the sand. I lay my head on his chest and savor the peaceful moment. We clarify that we will just be "friends" for the summer. We can reconvene next fall to talk about the future of our relationship. While I appear to agree with the decision to be just friends, my heart is not on board; however, because I've already told Elliott that I want to be just friends, I'm too embarrassed to tell him that I changed my mind.

I want to be exclusive over the summer. I like Elliott. I might even love him. I'm not sure fifteen-year-olds really know what love is, but if I had to label my feelings for him, I would say that I love him. I regret not telling him my true feelings about the mutual decision, and I wish I had made it clear to him that I really care about him. He means so much to me. I can't stand the thought of him with another girl.

The second I return home I regret going through with the conversation, but I can't call him and tell him I changed my mind because that would seem too flaky and ingenuine. I guess I will have to wait this one out.

Los Angeles → Peru: Friday, June 15th, 2018
Waking up at four in the morning isn't fun, yet I have no problem jumping out of bed. Once at the airport, everything runs smoothly. During my exchange, I will be attending Markham College in Peru. Markham College and Chadwick, my school in California,

are part of an organization of around 180 high schools worldwide called Round Square.

My flight is delayed twenty minutes because they have to bring in the plane from a remote part of the airport.

The first leg of the journey takes around four hours. I am forced to run through Fort Lauderdale because of a very brief layover, which is quite hectic. Thankfully, the flight from Fort Lauderdale to Lima is also delayed twenty minutes, so I arrive at the gate right as it is about to close. The people at the gate give me a weird look.

I attempt to sleep on the flight, but I'm bouncing up and down in my seat the entire time. I can't control my nerves.

In Lima, it takes a while for my bag to come.

While I am exiting the airport, I meet my host parents and my host sister Jay. I love my host parents, even though they don't speak much English, and Jay is hilarious and sweet. I think I am going to have a phenomenal trip.

At midnight, we drive to a fast-food chicken restaurant, and the food is spectacular. Restaurants must stay open really late here.

Even at midnight, the traffic in Lima is horrible.

I am glad to be away from my family. I love my family, but sometimes I feel like I need a break from them. My house is always chaotic because I have two younger siblings, and they are always entering my room. Jay tells me that I will have my own room. Having my own room, without two younger siblings constantly barging in, will be very peaceful.

Peru: Saturday, June 16th, 2018

I wake up at seven. Then Jay and I spend three hours just chilling around the house before we walk to a Chili's restaurant to watch the Peru versus Denmark World Cup game. We meet up with a few of Jay's friends, and some of them also have exchange students in tow. Everyone I meet seems to curse a lot. I am not used to cursing, but I have to keep up with them. I guess in order to fit in I should act like the other girls. They mostly speak in English, which is a blessing.

Jay does my makeup for the event we are attending this evening. I haven't worn makeup in a while. I am nervous about going to the event because I am not a fan of crowds. The event is called Rocking Russia because Russia is hosting the World Cup. I guess people just like the alliteration. By this point, I am completely out of energy; however, I can't show my exhaustion because we are planning to stay out for six hours.

Peru: Sunday, June 17th, 2018

Last night I met a guy named Vicente, who is one of

Jay's classmates at Markham College. At the end of the night, I kissed him, and now I'm nervous about seeing him in person tomorrow at school. Jay sends me a photo of us kissing, but I am too embarrassed to look at it.

Peru: Monday, June 18th, 2018

I go to all of Jay's classes. In Environmental Studies, we learn about the water cycle. The teacher calls on me. I correctly answer a question, and the teacher exclaims, "At least we have imported a smart one." I'm not sure how I feel about being described as "imported."

The exchange students ditch classes all the time, but I promise myself I won't. I am here to have the full Markham College student experience.

After Spanish, Jay has to write an essay, so I chill with the other exchange students in the library. There are twelve exchange students, and we have formed a little group.

After lunch, I have another Spanish class, but the exchange students are excused from the class, so we play the card game Spoons in the library.

Peru: Tuesday, June 19th, 2018

My bedroom has a serious ant infestation. I promise it's not my fault; they were here before I arrived.

I receive my personalized schedule! Markham College has an intelligent system where each student takes three standard classes and three honors classes, which in my mind eliminates the pressure of taking as many honors classes as possible. I wish my school was like this. I feel like in the United States there is so much pressure on the students to take as many APs or honors classes as possible. It isn't healthy.

I really miss Elliott. Even though I pushed Elliott into agreeing to just be friends, his enthusiasm for my recommendation stings. I haven't gotten a chance to talk to him since our conversation on the beach.

I want to spend more time with Jay and her friends because I find them to be more genuine than the exchange students, and I feel like Jay's friends like me more than the exchange students do. Being in a new place has given the exchange students the opportunity to reinvent themselves, which makes them feel ingenuine.

After school, Jay and I go shopping, and we get boba, a tea-based drink with chewy tapioca pearls. I need to branch out and meet new people. I FaceTime Camila, my closest friend from Chadwick. I also call Lola, another close friend of mine, who is my neighbor but doesn't attend my school.

Peru: Wednesday, June 20th, 2018

I love it here so much! My English teacher spends twenty minutes of class dissing America and Donald Trump. While I feel like I should take offense to some of the jokes, I can't because I am laughing so hard.

My host dad made me this delicious soup for lunch. I wish my parents could cook like him. My parents aren't bad cooks, but they tend to cook the same food over and over again. It's good to have a variety of food.

I lack self-confidence right now because I feel like the other exchange students aren't warming up to me. I wonder if I did something wrong.

I don't know what to do about Elliott. I keep thinking about him. I'm trying to focus on my experiences, but thoughts of Elliott keep slipping into my mind. I think I love him.

There is one exchange student that I feel like I'm bonding with: Desiree, an exchange student from Jordan. She seems friendly enough. She's two years older than me.

Jay and I attempt to watch two movies on Netflix. I manage to fall asleep during the first one, and I sleep through the second one.

Peru: Saturday, June 23rd, 2018

We chill at the house until three in the afternoon before we leave to go to a birthday party for one of Jay's friends. We play Never Have I Ever. I enjoy not losing for once. When I play Never Have I Ever with my friends at home, I often lose. I find it fascinating that a lot of the exchange students have reached certain sexual milestones in Peru. Why waste intimate experiences on a complete stranger, whom they probably will never see again?

After the birthday party ends, my host family and I go to Jockey, a huge mall, to buy clothes for Jay's brother, Gabe. I am not shopping for anything, so I walk around with Jay eating Cinnabon.

Jay and I attempt to finish the movie we were watching, but I fall asleep at midnight. Jay is sick, and I don't want to get sick; however, the likelihood of me avoiding the illness is very low because my immune system has been affected by my lack of sleep.

Peru: Sunday, June 24th, 2018

I sleep to ten in the morning because I am exhausted. Literally the second I wake up, Gabe walks into my room and apologizes for the shopping trip yesterday because he felt like it revolved totally around him. He has nothing to apologize for, but I tell him if it makes him feel better about himself, he can apologize to me all he wants. I find his apologetic behavior to be sweet.

I decide to do some ab-workouts to burn off some energy. In the Peruvian culture, they don't snack in-between meals like I am used to in the States. Because I am accustomed to snacking, I eat less during meals, and because during meals I am not used to stuffing myself, in-between meals I am famished.

We go to a shopping center, and I meet Jay's older sister and her British boyfriend. I have an internal laughing fit when I discover that Gabe is wearing all the clothes he bought yesterday. I am not sure why I find it amusing, but I also think it's charming.

I FaceTime Elliott while he is busy packing for Paris, which is strange because he leaves Saturday. Saturday is a week away. He acts like he doesn't want to talk to me. I wonder what thoughts are running through his head. He explains that he plans to leave his cell phone behind. I'm not sure if I believe that. Why doesn't he want to talk to me?

JULY

Peru: Monday, July 2nd, 2018

This morning Gabe tells me that I can talk to him anytime. I will probably take him up on that. He reminds me of Elliott. I miss Elliott so much. I hope he is doing well.

Desiree is talking to another exchange student, and when I walk up, they just fall silent. I feel ignored, and it hurts. I lack the confidence to walk to places alone.

During lunch, I sit with some of the other exchange students, yet I still feel like an outcast. One of the reasons I feel like an outcast is because the other exchange students are able to go to parties that my host parents won't allow me to go to. I don't blame my host parents because I understand that they are trying to protect me and keep me safe. Later today, a bunch of exchange students are going to a rave. I know the exchange students will talk about the parties on Monday, and I won't be able to add to the conversations.

Peru: Wednesday, July 4th, 2018

I feel like I am drifting away from Jay because she has been so busy. I feel bad that she never gets a break from me; however, I also feel conflicted because, on the other hand, I spend an enormous amount of time with the exchange students. It's difficult to balance out my time. Most of the exchange students are leaving next week, so I want to spend their remaining days with them.

Peru: Friday, July 6th, 2018

My host mom picks Jay and me up from school to drive to the Inca market, so I can buy gifts for my family. After visiting the Inca market, Jay feels bad because she knows that I am upset about not being allowed to go to a party. Jay and Gabe decide to walk to the mall with me to have Bembos and boba. That makes me feel better.

Bembos is a Peruvian, hamburger restaurant chain that in my opinion tops a lot of the burger chains in the United States.

We return home at around eleven at night. Then we go into Jay's room to play Mario Kart. At some point, we migrate into Gabe's room. At one in the morning, Jay decides she is tired. When Jay leaves, Gabe tries to teach me how to play Mario Odyssey. More accurately, he watches me suffer through it while I attempt to teach myself how to play. We stop playing video games and just start talking about life. He makes me think of Elliott. He is nineteen and hasn't kissed a girl, so I give him some girl advice. It reminds me of all the times when Elliott and I were just friends and I would give him advice. The nostalgia is kicking in. I do my best to hide it.

It is calming just talking to Gabe because, while I feel like the exchange students act so fake, he is genuine and authentic. I need to stop trying to be someone else, even if that means spending this last week without the other exchange students. I can't talk about Gabe to Jay because she gets jealous, and it's paramount that she understands he is just a friend. I don't tell Gabe much about myself, but I enjoy talking to him even if when we talk, we talk until the wee hours of the morning.

Peru: Saturday, July 7th, 2018

Jay wakes me up at ten to drive to Jockey. We spend four hours shopping.

Then we get ready for the Kermesse. The Kermesse is a carnival festival that Markham College hosts on their elementary school campus. My cellular data isn't working, so I am nervous. The Kermesse is amazing, although notably, I do spend fifty dollars on food that shouldn't be that expensive. I spend most of the time hanging out with Jay's friends rather than the exchange students. The exchange students can wear masks and be whoever they want to be because when they return home, it's not like anyone is going to know about their insane lives in Peru.

My host mom tells me I am not allowed to go out to a party after the Kermesse, even though I have been invited to two different ones. I feel left out because all the exchange students are going to parties, but I respect my host parents and I appreciate that they have taken me under their care and protection.

Peru: Tuesday, July 10th, 2018

At the end of the exchange, the exchange students buy a Peruvian flag, and they try to have as many people sign it as possible. It's a Round Square tradition. I bought my flag while I was at the Inca market.

I spend a few hours working on Jay's gift. I am putting seventy-two notes into a bottle. Each little note is either a thank-you note, a remember-when-we-did-this note, or an inside joke. I hope she likes it.

Desiree has already kissed sixteen people so far in Peru, and she has a goal of kissing four more to leave with a solid twenty. I could never set a goal like that for myself. It would make me feel like a bad person.

Jay and I get boba for the third consecutive day. We are facing a bit of a dilemma. Both of the toilets in the house are currently clogged, so we have to get boba in order to use the restroom in the shopping mall.

Peru: Wednesday, July 11th, 2018

I keep thinking about everything I have to do at home: take my driver's license course, have my sweet sixteen party, hang with friends, and spend quality time with my family again. All my thoughts centered around the future are preventing me from living in the moment. I have a bit of free time. I don't know what to do with myself. I have been stuck spending time alone with my thoughts. I have found that journaling releases some of the angst trapped within me. I am going to try to start journaling more frequently.

Peru: Friday, July 13th, 2018

Friday the thirteenth has an air of bad mojo. In biology, one of my classmates invites me to her house.

My plan is to celebrate a friend's birthday at Larcomar and then Uber to my classmate's house to hang out.

I have to sit through a two-hour assembly, and I nearly fall asleep. It is my last day at Markham College, and I am going to miss it. I loved my exchange experience.

After school, Jay and I get boba and Bembos. Jay has a friend visiting from the United States, and she wants to spend some quality time with her. Jay and I split up and go our separate ways. The Uber to Larcomar takes fifty minutes, and I am only there for forty minutes before I go to my classmate's house.

Peru: Friday, July 13th
(Written from court documents on April 4th, 2020)
I didn't journal for the night of the thirteenth because I didn't want to remember any of it. I feel like I owe it to my readers to include a description of the night of the rape because it demonstrates how such a short period of time can dramatically change someone's life. I had to look back through the notes that I wrote for the testimony I gave in August of 2018. I crafted this entry using those notes.

At 9:45 at night, we leave my classmate's house to go to a party. For the next forty minutes, I hang out with my friends.

Around 10:30, Vicente approaches me. (I know who he is because I had met him at the Rocking Russia event about a month earlier, and we had kissed at that event.) Then Vicente and I walk from the balcony to the back-patio area. We walk into the laundry room where we start kissing. I leave a few minutes later to go hang out with my friends.

After some time, I go to the bathroom. As I am leaving the bathroom, Vicente approaches me and offers me a sip from a bottle of Pisco that he has been carrying in the inside pocket of his jacket. The bottle is open, but I can tell that it hasn't been drunken from. He offers me the bottle. I drink two sips. I enjoy talking to him too much to notice that he doesn't drink from the bottle, nor does he offer the bottle to anyone else.

I walk away from him to talk to my friends. Two minutes later he approaches me again and asks if I want to go to the back room. By this point it is around 11:00, and I am starting to feel dizzy. I don't have much recollection of the timing after this point, but I have fragmented memories.

I collapse on the bed and drop my purse on the floor. I am lying on the bed with my legs hanging off the side. Vicente unzips my pants and pulls them down so that they lay around my ankles. He removes my sweatshirt and shirt. My phone is next to me on the bed, but my muscles feel too weak to reach out and grab it. Vicente pulls down my underwear and takes off his pants. Then he positions himself on the bed above me and penetrates me vaginally.

While he was violating me, I feel scared and confused. I am incapacitated. The moments I remember most vividly are moments of excruciating pain. I had been a virgin prior to this point in time. As he thrust into me, I slide off the bed, so for his convenience, he moves me such that I am lying with my head by the headboard on the bed. He continues raping me. My head slams into the headboard every time he thrusts himself inside me. My eyes are closed, but I can feel his presence above me. It feels like I am being ripped apart. I tell him to stop, but he continues until he is done.

When he is done, he walks away into the bathroom. I don't remember how long I was lying on the bed, but when he returns, he is fully clothed. He pulls up my pants and zips them. Then he sits me up on my knees. He removes his penis from his pants. I keep falling sideways on the bed, so he grabs my hair to hold up my head as he rapes me orally. I gag as he thrusts himself into me. I feel like I am going to vomit. I can feel the bile rising up in my throat.

At some point, Vicente leaves the room, and I lay on the bed for a while alone. When I regain the ability to move, I text my host sister to pick me up. She did around 12:15 in the morning. I stand up, even though I feel weak. I retrieve my shirt and sweatshirt that

Vicente had thrown on the floor. I put on my sweat-shirt, and I put my shirt in my purse.

When Jay's mom picks me up, Jay and her brother are in the car. I don't talk on the way home. I vow to myself to never tell a soul about what had happened to me.

Peru: Saturday, July 14th, 2018

I don't want to write or think about last night. After breakfast, some of Jay's friends come over. We go out for boba again. It is nice to see them one last time.

I call my mom and come to the conclusion that I can never tell her about last night. What the hell am I saying? I can never tell anyone. I'll pretend nothing happened. In a few years, I will be out of the house and on my own.

I give Jay her gift, and she loves it. I still have to get Gabe to sign my flag, but I doubt that will happen because he doesn't believe in the whole flag-signing thing. He thinks it's superficial and petty.

Peru: Sunday, July 15th, 2018

My alarm clock wakes me up at ten in the morning; meanwhile, Jay is still sleeping.

For our Sunday lunch, my host dad makes ceviche, which is the best meal I have had this trip. As an appetizer, we have clams with lemon juice and melted cheese; they are pretty good considering that I don't normally like clams.

After lunch, Jay and I decide to get boba, and we walk to the mall. I haven't told Jay about the rape, but how am I supposed to tell her?

I receive a WhatsApp message from Desiree saying that Vicente is telling people we had sex. I vent to Jay about that, and I tell her what Vicente is saying isn't true. I hate that not a single person knows the whole truth. No one is going to ever find out.

Peru: Monday, July 16th, 2018

I have bread with avocado for breakfast: it tastes good because I made it myself.

On the night of the thirteenth, during the party, I think Vicente had a condom. Why can't I remember? My mind is foggy. What if I am pregnant? I'm actually looking forward to my next period.

I had a terrible nightmare last night. I got pregnant with the rapist's child, and I had to raise it all by myself. In my nightmare, my family abandoned me, and I was living in a tiny shack watching an infant scream.

My family is coming to Peru at the end of my exchange, and we will spend around two weeks sightseeing in Cuzco. My host family warns me about potentially getting altitude sickness when my family and I visit Cuzco.

After lunch, I play a round of Mario Kart with Gabe. Even though he has finals next week, he takes time away from studying to hang out with me. I am going to miss him. My parents and siblings are flying to Lima in two days. I start packing. My exchange is coming to an end.

Peru: Wednesday, July 18th, 2018

One more day until my sixteenth birthday! I have to say today is bittersweet. Jay and I visit her sister's apartment. We help her sister for an hour while she wraps up paintings.

Then we go to the MALI museum and spend an hour looking at art. Truthfully, it is kind of boring.

When I think about that night at the party, I keep denying what happened. Why do I have to justify it? It happened. I didn't give consent, and I guarantee that I told him to stop. I can't tell anyone. Anyway, my exchange is over. The past has to stay behind me. If I am pregnant, I am screwed, but unless that happens, I won't tell anyone. I can't tell anyone!

I walk with Jay to get boba again. I also buy flowers for my host family.

Around seven at night, my parents come to pick me up. We check into the hotel, which is right by the main square in Miraflores. We walk to dinner, and I give my family a tour of the square and the murals.

It is great to see my family after so long. I especially missed my brother and sister.

I pray that my period comes soon. Should I come to terms with what happened, or should I bury the past?

Peru: Thursday, July 19th, 2018

Well, it's my birthday! As happy as I am, I am equally distraught because I have to leave Jay.

I feel like I am on the verge of telling my mom my secret. She keeps saying that I'm old enough to handle being on my own, but obviously I am not. The past is the past, and it shouldn't haunt me, but it does. With the exception of being stuck in my own head, my birthday is okay.

Jay and my family spend the whole day visiting various malls: La Rambla, Jockey, and Larcomar.

For my birthday dinner, my host family takes my family out to dinner at a fancy restaurant located at the end of a pier. I predict that the dinner atmosphere will be awkward because my parents don't speak any Spanish and my host parents speak very little English; however, the dinner goes surprisingly well because Jay, Gabe, and I are able to translate for the parents.

Peru: Friday, July 20th, 2018

I have already been in Peru for five weeks. This morning, my family and I wake up at 4:30. The early awakening is awful because I had been haunted by flashbacks of the rape, which kept me up until two in the morning. Despite the flashbacks that kept me up, I don't remember any of my dreams so that is a relief. All of my dreams have been traumatizing lately.

The flight to Cuzco is delayed forty-five minutes, which is a blessing because I am able to take a two-hour nap. The tour guide picks us up at the airport, and even though I only spend part of the day with the tour guide, I think he is spectacular. We visit an alpaca farm. I have the opportunity to take selfies with the alpacas. Some of the alpacas don't like taking selfies. I receive a few head butts from some antisocial alpacas.

Then we drive to the Sacred Valley. I am starting to feel queasy because of the elevation. The alpaca farm is located 13,000 feet above sea level. Thankfully, our hotel is at only 9,000 feet above sea level. My mom and I eat dinner together, just the two of us, and guess what I have! Alpaca steak!

If I end up getting pregnant, then I'll have to tell my mom. In this hypothetical situation, I would want to have an abortion, but there is no use thinking about that now. Thankfully, my family isn't religious, and we are pro-choice, so if I were to get pregnant, my parents would support my decision. That's the worst-case scenario. I'm probably not pregnant.

Peru: Monday, July 23rd, 2018

I wake up with no energy. I try to figure out why. My conclusion is because it has been weeks since I have truly exercised. I lack energy, or maybe I am just lazy. I also think I am gaining weight. I should eat less.

My family is going on a bike ride, but my sister and I opt not to go, so as an alternative, we explore the hotel. I attempt to exercise. I also drink five strawberry juices. I have to take advantage of the easy access to strawberry juice because it is difficult to find strawberry juice at restaurants in the United States.

I have to pack because tomorrow we are taking a train to Machu Picchu! The elevation is affecting me, and I haven't felt one hundred percent since I arrived in the Sacred Valley. My sister and I eat lunch together because my mom goes to get a massage and my father and brother leave the hotel to fly my brother's drone.

My secret has to stay with just me and me alone. I have to learn from my past mistakes, but at some point, I have to move on! I am so thankful for the life I live, and now, I have managed to mess it up. It's time to bury the past.

Peru: Tuesday, July 24th, 2018

It has been eleven days since the rape, and my period is eight days late. My period is rarely late. I think I am pregnant. I finally crack. My mom finds out my secret, and she reacts better than I could have hoped for.

I am crying in the back seat of the van, and she comes up to me and just hugs me. I don't want to talk, and she knows that. She asks me, "Mackenzie, were you raped?" My tears intensify, and I looked up at her. She knows. It is a mother's intuition. My mom handles everything so well, but I think now it's going to haunt her too.

I realize that I have to talk about the rape, so I can move on. I'm so thankful for my mother. She stops at a pharmacy and buys me two pregnancy tests.

Then we board a train to Machu Picchu. Machu Picchu is everything I imagined it would be even though I have a terrible headache, and my complaining causes my whole family to leave early.

My mom and I wait two hours in line to take the bus back down to the hotel. Once we are back down at the hotel, we eat dinner as a family and then play Euchre. My dad and I win again, just like last night! I don't want my dad to find out what happened to me, but I can tell that what I shared with my mom is affecting her.

I need to tell my dad about the rape soon, so he can help provide the support that I can't provide for my mom. It's ironic that I am more concerned for my mom than myself. I can handle the past.

I text Jay for a while. I miss her, but we are going to hang out when I fly back to Lima.

Hallelujah! I just took a pregnancy test. It was negative.

Peru: Friday, July 27th, 2018

Last night, my mom and I told my dad about the rape. I feel much better today because I know that now my mom can receive the support she needs, and I don't have to continue hiding my true feelings from my dad.

I had another nightmare last night. In my dream, I was in a setting similar to that of the night I was raped, and everywhere I looked, I was surrounded by people who looked like Vicente. They all had different outfits, but every time I looked at one of their faces, I saw Vicente's face.

My brother, sister, dad, and I drive an hour out of Cuzco to see ruins from a civilization that predated the Incas. We walk around the ruins for about an hour, and then we drive to a church. After touring the church, we go to a small museum where we see human skulls that had been elongated because the Incas used to tie pieces of wood around infant nobles' heads, which caused their craniums to deform.

When we return to the hotel, my parents and I have a meeting to talk about the next steps. We decide that we want to fight for justice. My parents don't want me to regret not doing so in the future. Frankly, I am a little skeptical about attempting to get justice because Peru is very corrupt, and I doubt the case will go anywhere. During my exchange, I learned that Markham College students tend to be wealthy and have ample connections. Considering that my family and I are foreigners, the likelihood of having a fair trial is miniscule. Why even try?

While the rest of my family is touring Cuzco, my mom stays back at the hotel so she can call the United States Embassy. The lady who answers the phone explains to my mom that they have had many instances of students using ketamine as a date-rape drug. Ketamine is a common roofie. Ketamine is the only roofie that doesn't render the victim fully unconscious, which would make sense in my case because I only recall fragments of that night.

My brother is very intuitive and becomes suspicious because my mother and father spend so much time texting. In his investigation, he asks my dad for his phone and sneakily takes screenshots of text messages between my parents. One of the texts between my parents talks about needing to find a criminal lawyer. My brother calls a meeting with my sister and me. He asks us to help him investigate why our parents are texting about finding a criminal lawyer.

Obviously, I know what is happening, so I tell my dad about my brother's little investigation. I don't want my siblings to find out that I was drugged and raped, so we devise a plan. My dad is going to call my brother, sister, and me to our parents' hotel room, to explain why taking screenshots of another person's phone is an invasion of privacy and so on.

While my father is lecturing my brother and sister, my mom breaks down and starts crying. Seeing my mom cry on account of a situation that involves me, is too difficult to bear. I stand up and tell my siblings the truth rendering both of them speechless. Both my parents have been so supportive, and I love them so much. Now the whole family knows the truth.

Peru: Sunday, July 29th, 2018

We land in Lima around 3:30 in the afternoon. I have about thirty minutes to relax before the lawyers arrive at the hotel to meet us. I am jittery. My lawyer and four other members of his legal team enter the hotel room. Sandro Monteblanco, my lawyer and the head of the firm, introduces himself first. Upon first impression, Sandro Monteblanco seems like a stand-up, intelligent lawyer who speaks fluent English, which helps calm my nerves.

I make my mom, my dad, and my siblings leave the room while I recount my story. I have figured out why I have blank spots in my memory. I remember that Vicente had handed me a bottle of Pisco, and I took two sips. It was only after drinking the Pisco that I felt lightheaded, dizzy, and a little nauseous. My parents and lawyers think that I had been drugged. That would explain all of the blank spots in my memory. The lawyers speak amongst themselves in Spanish, but I understand every word.

Sandro Monteblanco tells me very politely that when I retell the story later to the detective, I have to be very precise with my diction. For example, rather than saying he fucked me, which is the language I am most comfortable using, I have to say he penetrated me vaginally. It is difficult to wrap my head around the change in terminology because I never use those phrases in daily life. After spending a few hours describing the rape and answering various questions, my mom accompanies the lawyers and me to the police station. I explain the rape to the detective while Sandro Monteblanco translates from English to Spanish so that the detective can simultaneously type up a police report. While I recount my story, I feel numb.

Then we drive about twenty minutes in a police car to a place where I have a medical exam to see if there is any internal damage. The rape occurred sixteen days ago, so I am convinced they won't find anything. My mom and I are escorted into a compound with a rectangular, open-aired courtyard in the center. My lawyer is prohibited from entering the compound. The most stressful part of the evening is taking the medical exam because the doctor won't let my lawyer into the compound, and I don't know enough Spanish to talk about private subjects. It is a real struggle trying to answer very personal questions in Spanish. The doctor also has me sign a bunch of documents, but with the stress and my lack of Spanish vocabulary for legal words, I have no idea what the documents say, which freaks my mom out. I have to calm her down to the point where she agrees to sign all the documents. It's stressful. They only teach you so much in Spanish class.

Next, we drive to another location to take a toxicology test to see if there are any roofie drugs in my system. I return to the hotel around midnight. I am emotionally drained, but I am physically amped up, and I proceed to stay up all night. I haven't cried once today. I feel as cold as ice. It is almost as if I don't have any energy to express any emotions, or maybe I just don't have any emotions to express. Now I just feel numb.

AUGUST

Maine: Wednesday, August 1st, 2018

I am in Porter, Maine! My mother's family has a 200-year-old farmhouse out in the middle of nowhere, where all my cousins meet up for a few weeks every summer. My father has returned to Los Angeles.

Today is a pleasant day. I wake up at 9:30 in the morning. The rest of the family is sitting and talking downstairs. I relax, read some books, and run some errands with my grandma. We drive to the hardware store to buy soil because we are planting a garden.

After that, I help my grandma by rain-proofing the house, unloading the dishwasher, and playing with her new kitten. The new kitten loves playing with people, but she's a little violent. I now have an array of scratches on my arms. Also, the kitten has fleas, and thankfully, she's been given medication for them, so they drop dead all over the place.

I clean out the cabin located along a hidden trail descending into the woods from the farmhouse. I dispose of all the mouse droppings, hornet nests, and dirt. It is a gross job, but someone has to do it. In the old dresser, I find a family of five mice whom I proceed to chase out of the cabin.

Maine: Friday, August 3rd, 2018

From the upstairs room in the farmhouse, I can hear all the conversations happening below me, so I am awoken around eight. I was in the middle of a nightmare, so I remember it. I was running, and I was being chased by a black figure towards fiery inferno. The whole time I was running, I could hear someone laughing.

The lawyers are working on the case, but I receive some devastating news. We have to return to Lima, and I have to give my testimony on August 24th. Darn it, that is the day I am scheduled to take driving test. If I pass, I could get my license. Nevertheless, I want Vicente to be put in prison because he doesn't deserve to roam free with the potential of assaulting other women, so if I have to return to Lima to testify, I will do it in a heartbeat!

Maine: Tuesday, August 7th, 2018

Camila, my closest friend, has flown in from Los Angeles to spend a week with us

One of the mouse traps got set off in the house. The mouse is already injured. I have to do the ethical thing and hit it in the head with a rock to put it out of its misery, and now Camila thinks I am a murderer.

I tell Camila about the rape. She is shocked, but she does a good job remaining calm. I have to say that there is no way to sugarcoat the fact that I have been drugged and raped. Every time I tell someone my story, the introduction is, "This summer I was drugged and raped." I hate having to tell people that.

I have missed Camila, and I think she likes Maine. Camila and I decide that we will sleep in the cabin that I cleaned up a few days ago, so we can talk and catch up. In the cabin, Camila and I embark on a spider-killing rampage. It's not that I enjoy murdering spiders, but Camila isn't a fan of them. I am just helping her out.

Camila and I make a nightly video, which is a tradition we have when we travel together. Each night of our trip, we make a video to recap our day, and we add any inside jokes that have been created that day. It's a way to reflect but also to laugh off any challenges we have recently faced. Plus, we will have videos to look back on in the future.

Maine: Wednesday, August 8th, 2018

Camila and I wake up early so she can go for a run while I have my daily cup of coffee. Afterwards, we go over to my grandma's house. Currently, my grandma is in Ohio visiting friends, but she is letting us use her kitchen. We also have to take care of her kitten. Camila, my sister, and I spend the day making jewelry and cooking. I make mac and cheese in a kettle because I can't find a pot.

In the evening, my mom gets mad at me. She is so devastated that I was raped that she is projecting her guilt onto me. I don't want to deal with her, so I yell at her, which isn't very productive. She gets so mad that she makes me sleep in the cabin alone. She makes Camila sleep upstairs with her and my sister. I fall asleep quickly despite being angry and frustrated.

Maine: Thursday, August 9th, 2018

My mom isn't doing so well. She concludes that she has been blaming herself for the whole rape situation, so we end up talking about it for thirty minutes. While we are talking, she can't stop crying. She is more upset about the rape than me. I guess that's because I don't know how I am supposed to feel about it. She asks me if I want to go back to Los Angeles. I tell her that because Camila is here I have to stay. I make my mom promise not to tell my aunt and my uncle about the rape. I feel like my mom doesn't want to lie to her siblings. Because my mom has nobody to vent to here, the truth is eating her up inside.

It's my uncle's birthday. I go to my grandma's house to bake a chocolate cheesecake. I don't realize that you have to melt the chocolate chips and then mix them into the cheesecake batter, so the cheesecake turns into a chocolate chip cheesecake. I've promised my grandma her kitchen will be spotless after baking, so Camila and I spend two hours cleaning it up.

When we return to the farm, Camila starts to cook dinner. I am feeling lazy, so I just read a book on the couch.

The fear of having to return to Lima soon is eating away at me. I don't want to go back, but I have to, not just for myself, but for all the other potential sexual assault victims of my rapist.

Maine: Friday, August 10th, 2018

It's Friday. I sleep in. Camila and I decide to go fishing. We borrow my neighbor friend's fishing rods. Camila manages to get her hook stuck in a tree. Despite not catching any fish, we lose around ten worms. After two hours of trying to fish, we just lie down for an hour on the side of the road because both of us are too tired to move. We return back to the farm where we untangle the fishing rods.

Camila and I stay up until one in the morning because Camila has a ton of energy. I am not going to complain because normally I am the hyper one at night.

Maine: Saturday, August 11th, 2018

Camila and I have to go to my grandma's house so we can finish cleaning her kitchen. We don't want her to complain about anything being out of place. We end up stranded at the house for about three hours. We could walk around two miles back to the farmhouse, but Camila hurt her knee, so that isn't an option. We are starving, so I make mac and cheese. Camila manages to drop a bowl of frozen blueberries. It is quite a struggle. Wow, when I live in a dorm room in college, it's going to be chaotic. At least I am getting a little taste of my potential experiences now. We finally manage to make it back to the farm, and we continue to lounge in our laziness.

As usual, Camila and I stay up until midnight.

One thing I find funny is that Gabe texts me more than Jay. It's a little strange because in Peru I spent way more time with Jay than Gabe.

My mom is progressively becoming more stressed because her guilt about my rape is intensifying. Each day, it gets worse. It hurts me to see my family members beat their heads against the wall because of something that I told them. Frankly, it might have been better if I just hadn't told them. If that were the case, at least I would be the only one dealing with the pain, rather than seeing my entire family suffer on my account. I don't know how I should feel. I don't feel any emotions about the rape. Is that normal?

Maine → Duxbury: Sunday, August 12th, 2018
It's our last day in Maine, and we leave around four in the afternoon. Prior to our departure, Camila and I go to sweep out my grandma's house. During the car ride, I spend the time knitting a scarf. About two hours into the drive, my sister decides that she needs to use the restroom, but due to the fact that we are in the middle of nowhere, it takes thirty minutes to locate a bathroom. It is a struggle, but we finally find a burger place that looks like an old-fashioned diner with red plastic-covered couches and low tables. Then we drive another hour and arrive at our friend's house in Duxbury, Massachusetts.

Duxbury: Monday, August 13th, 2018
Camila decides to swim, and the water is warmer than I thought it would be. The house that we are staying at is right on the beach.

Camila and I play monopoly with the kids whose parents own the house. After dinner, these random other kids show up, and no one wants to socialize, but my mom thinks we are being impolite. She tells me to go hang out with the other kids. I don't feel like spending time with kids who are four years younger than me, so I tell my mom that I will just stay in my room. My mom isn't too enthusiastic about that idea, and somehow the situation catapults into the two of us yelling at each other.

Like me, my sister doesn't want to play with the other kids, so she joins the fray, which ends with my mom and sister crying. Their feelings stem from their guilt surrounding what happened to me in Peru. I hate seeing everyone I love suffering, and I blame myself for their suffering: Had I not told them what had happened to me, they wouldn't be upset. It would have been so much better if I had just kept my mouth shut. My mom is taking this even worse than I am. I just feel numb about everything.

Camila ends up freaking out because she realizes that she too has her own family problems to deal with. By this point, it's midnight. Camila is crying, so we decide to take a long walk. We don't return to the house until two in the morning.

Duxbury→ Los Angeles: Tuesday, August 14th, 2018

A lawnmower wakes me up at nine in the morning. I could have slept for a few more hours. I have three huge cups of coffee. Camila tells my mom about her family problems. I think that there are some stories that must be shared with the ones we are close to. Everyone has problems in their lives, and people shouldn't compare their problems to other peoples' issues because there shouldn't be a competition to see who has the most messed-up life. All you can do is rely on the people close to you to help you see the light at the end of the tunnel.

My mom's friend approaches me and tells me to stay strong, and she gives me a rock on which, in black sharpie, she has written *strength* on one side and *calm* on the other. My mom's friend is kind, and I can tell that my mom admires her. My mom must have told her about the rape. I am annoyed because my mom promised me that she wouldn't tell anyone without my permission. She didn't ask for my permission to tell her friend.

Our flight is delayed, and my sister is not very enthusiastic about that. She wants to get home as soon as possible, and I don't blame her. It has been a long trip.

Los Angeles: Wednesday, August 15th, 2018

I am finally home. My room was repainted while I was in Maine, so everything has been moved off my desk. I have to put everything back in its rightful place. I also start to pack for my school's grade-wide camping trip. Assuming we can come home from

Peru right after the testimony, I'll be able to go on the camping trip. I make a list of stuff I have to do before leaving for Peru. I like to be organized, and making lists is actually relatively calming. I don't think about the rape at all. I tell Jay and Gabe that I am coming back to Peru. I am sure that they have to be suspicious at this point because they don't know about the rape.

Vicente hasn't hired a lawyer, which my lawyer finds strange.

Los Angeles: Thursday, August 16th, 2018

I've been home for two days this entire summer. I go to the doctor's office to get tested for sexually transmitted diseases since I can't remember whether or not the rapist used a condom. I give a lot of blood. I am not a fan of needles. I can feel my heart pumping in my chest while they are extracting the blood. Just to be on the safe side, my doctor wants me to take an HIV medication to preemptively prevent myself from getting it. The medicine sucks because I feel extremely nauseous after taking it.

I go to therapy with my mom. Overall, I think the therapy session goes well, but my mom spends the time crying non-stop. I explain to the therapist that when she's crying, I feel like I should be the strong one in the family, which is easy to do because I feel numb. I don't know how to explain the feeling that I have been experiencing since the rape. I feel like I should be feeling anger, sadness, or frustration that my family is breaking down around me, but I don't. I try to act as I would if I were capable of expressing emotions, but it's hard without being able to actually process any emotions.

After therapy, my dad picks me up, and we go to REI to buy gear for my camping trip.

I have a long FaceTime with Camila just to make sure that she's okay.

There are many things that I'm looking forward to doing when I'm in Lima. Maybe I'll get to see some of my friends. I have a lot on my mind right now, and I am trying to decide whether or not I should tell my host family about the rape. I realize that if I go back, I will have to see them, but how much do they need to know? How public do I want to make this situation?

When I talked to my lawyers in Lima, I recorded the fifty-seven-minute-long conversation. I haven't been able to bring myself to listen to it yet, but I know I will have to at some point and take notes in order to prep for my testimony.

Los Angeles: Friday, August 17th, 2018

My dad and I go shopping for a new backpack for next year. We go to this cute, little farmers market. I buy some watermelon juice! Afterwards, we go to Staples to buy school supplies.

I babysit my neighbor, Rafe. I started babysitting Rafe when I was twelve because his parents bought my parents' old house, which is two houses down the street from where I live now. It has been incredible to watch Rafe grow up. When I first started babysitting him, he was in diapers, and next year he is starting kindergarten at Chadwick. While I am babysitting Rafe, we decide to go for a walk and run through any sprinklers in people's yards that are turned on. It is a blast!

When Rafe's mom returns, she gives me an abalone necklace for my birthday. She tells me it was handmade in Lunada Bay, and she wants me to always have something from home on my travels. She tells me that each necklace is unique, like me. She hopes I will continue to be the unique, wonderful person I am. I don't think I am that wonderful or unique, but of course I am not going to tell her that. I have to keep my self-deprecating thoughts to myself.

Los Angeles: Saturday, August 18th, 2018

My neighbor friend Lola and I hang out at her house. For some reason, I am annoyed with her, but I don't know why. We mostly talk about her cross-country trip and the drama that she encountered while on that trip.

I spend an hour talking to my mom. I just feel annoyed with people right now. I don't know why, but at least I feel something.

I go over to Camila's, and her family takes me out to Green Temple, our favorite vegetarian restaurant. She told her family about what happened to me over the summer. I love Camila's parents, but it feels strange knowing that they know I was raped. I hope they don't think of me any differently.

I am freaking out about returning to Peru. The truth of the situation is starting to hit me. I don't want to go back. I don't know what emotions I should feel, and I don't know how to act.

To make matters worse, I think I still like Elliott.

Los Angeles: Sunday, August 19th, 2018

I slept over at Camila's last night. I actually slept better than normal, and I didn't have any nightmares, which was a blessing. We decide to go to the movie theater to watch *Crazy Rich Asians* with Lola. I cry on three separate occasions. I have all this pent-up energy. I should go for a run to let some of it out. I just feel angry at everything. What is happening to me? I feel like I am going to explode.

Los Angeles: Monday, August 20th, 2018
It's Monday, but it doesn't feel like Monday. Maybe that's because it's still summer. I made plans to hang out with Camila, but I just feel like being by myself, so I cancel the plans.

I watch a movie on YouTube, and then I go to a Yellow Vase cafe with my mom for lunch. I also manage to get into a fight with my sister because according to her I take up too much "mom time." I feel bad for my sister because I agree with her that my parents are directing all their attention towards me and the case. It must be difficult for my little sister, who is only twelve years old.

I have therapy. I briefly fill in my therapist on what happened to me over the summer, but mostly we talk about how to make this next week in Peru manageable. I like to box away my feelings because I consider myself to be a logical-thinking person. I try not to base my decisions on emotions.

I listen to the fifty-seven minutes of me describing the rape. I also make a list of key points I want to highlight. I am flying to Peru tomorrow. Wish me luck!

Peru: Wednesday, August 22nd, 2018
We arrived in Peru around midnight. This morning my mom calls the hotel room to wake me up because she left to meet with Jay's mom for breakfast to tell

her about the rape. Jay's mom asks if she can see me, so my mom tells me to get ready. I am super nervous. I don't know what to say to her. It's too early in the morning to see the look of pity people tend to give me after they find out. It's hard enough to start a conversation with, "Oh, by the way, I was drugged and raped." The meeting with my host mom goes well. She is super supportive.

I don't have a chance to work out because I go over to Jay's house. Jay's mom, Gabe, Jay, my mom and I go out for dinner. It is good to catch up with Jay. She updates me on all the new gossip at Markham College.

Peru: Thursday, August 23rd, 2018

I wake up at around noon, just in time for lunch. I spend two hours writing down everything that I can use for my testimony tomorrow. I am nervous, and I just feel angry at the entire world. I want Vicente to go and die in a hole! I also write down all the questions I want to ask Sandro Monteblanco.

After my fourth cup of coffee, I slink downstairs. Sandro Monteblanco comes over, and we discuss the case. I don't feel ready whatsoever. At this point, I just want to go home. I like my lawyer. I believe he is preparing me to the greatest extent that he can. One strategy he wants me to employ is if I get asked unfair or irrelevant questions during the testimony, he wants me to throw back the questions at the defense lawyers. My favorite comeback Sandro Monteblanco gives me is, "Well, have you ever been raped before?"

What the testimony will consist of:
◊ A two-hour psychological exam
◊ Around three hours of answering questions spoken by the psychologist then translated by a translator (includes cross-examination)

Remember for the testimony:
◊ I will be recorded
◊ Due to having a translator, the flow will be slightly interrupted
◊ Don't use the F-word at all
◊ Say vaginal penetration
◊ Be very descriptive and describe events in detail
◊ Don't answer a question with "I don't know."
◊ Instead say "Let me recall."
◊ Showing anger is a good thing
◊ Crying is a good thing
◊ Tell the story in first person
◊ Good eye contact

◊ It's okay to go back if I forget to add some information

Good phrases to use during the testimony:

◊ The word "RAPE" must be ingrained in the prosecutor's head

◊ "I don't understand the question. Is there something wrong with (kissing, talking to boys, etc...)?"

◊ "Even though we kissed, he didn't have the authority (right) to rape me."

◊ Directed to the prosecutor: "Are you insinuating that I wanted to be raped?"

◊ "Well, have you ever been raped?"

My conclusion:

◊ I came here to Peru to study.

◊ I came here to meet new people and experience a new culture.

◊ I didn't come here to be raped.

Peru: Friday, August 24th, 2018

The trial day has arrived. I leave the hotel at eight in the morning because I have to be at the Fiscalía, the equivalent of the district attorney's office, by ten.

When we get there, we meet up with an agent assigned to us by the United States Embassy.

Vicente's defense lawyers, which he has just hired according to Sandro Monteblanco, bring their own translator and psychologist, which makes me nervous. The Fiscalía is already supplying a psychologist and a translator. I am escorted into a little room where I meet the prosecutor, the translator, and the psychologist who is going to be asking me questions in the interview chamber. The prosecutor has a mug with children printed on it. I ask her questions about her kids in broken Spanish, and I think that she likes me despite the fact that there is a prominent language barrier.

In the questioning chamber, there are tiny, colorful chairs, probably because the room is normally used for cases that involve families. I feel like the psychologist is doing a great job filtering questions from both councils.

Some of the questions I am asked, irritate me. For example, the psychologist asks, "What were you wearing the night of your rape?" First off, even if I was wearing slutty clothing, that wouldn't give anyone the right to rape me. Besides, I was wearing jeans and a sweatshirt.

After around a half an hour, I can see tears in the psychologist's eyes. The questioning only lasts around two hours. We go into the psychologist's office for the psychological examination. She asks me to draw a few pictures: a boy, a girl, a person in the rain, and a picture of my family.

Then I have to answer about 150 true or false questions, which I feel are pretty dumb. It takes an extremely long time because all the questions are in Spanish, and even though I can translate them myself, the translator insists on translating the questions into English before I give her an answer.

We leave at around 5:30 in the evening, but as we are leaving, the prosecutor is moved to another case, or, we theorize, fired from our case, which is strange. Sandro Monteblanco seems concerned. He explains that this never happens, especially in a minor's case. Could this be a case of bribery? I wouldn't put this past the rapist's family.

Brief Summary of Peru's Criminal Justice System

In Peru, there are two stages of prosecution. The first is directed by a prosecutor, and if he or she deems there is enough evidence for the case to go to court, the case goes to court. If our prosecutor rules in favor of the defense, we can appeal, like in the United States, and a superior prosecutor will review the case. If at either stage the prosecutor or superior prosecutor decides that there is enough evidence to take the case to court, the case is brought to the first stage of the court system. The first stage has a single judge, and if they rule in our favor then Vicente will be sentenced; however, like in the United States, the defense council can appeal. If either side appeals, the case goes to a panel of three judges that review the case and issue a verdict. If the case is appealed again, it goes to the Supreme Court of Peru and is reviewed by a panel of seven judges. Unlike the United States, there isn't a jury at any point in the process.

Peru: Saturday, August 25th, 2018

We find out that we have to stay in Peru because they want to give me another psychological exam on Monday. Darn, I guess I am going to miss my grade-wide camping trip. What am I going to tell my friends at home?

I don't feel safe here. I have this little voice in my head that is trying to convince me that my rapist's family will send an assassin after me to kill me. I guess I am just that scared.

In the afternoon, Gabe comes over. We play Mario Kart. We walk to Larcomar. Having Gabe around allows me to have more freedom because my mom considers him to be an adult. He is nineteen, so legally he is an adult. Afterwards, Gabe and I go to the lounge and talk about life. I am opening up to him more about the rape, but I can tell that he doesn't want to talk about it because he cares about me so much.

We come up with a bunch of inside jokes while listening to 70's music. I think he has a little crush on me. If only I didn't like Elliott.

Peru: Sunday, August 26th, 2018

I bought a new journal before I left for this trip, but it looks like I am going to work backwards in my current one because I left my new journal at home. When I journal, I always write on the right page and leave the left page blank. I try to write a page a day, unless something exciting happens, and then I write more.

I haven't anticipated being in Peru as long as I have been. I meet up with two of my Peruvian friends from Markham College, and we walk around Larcomar while eating crepes. I tell my Peruvian friends about the rape and request that they spread the word that Vicente raped me. Because he is a Markham College student, my friends and the other girls at Markham College are in danger. My friends text a group chat with every single girl in their grade and tell them that an exchange student was drugged and raped.

I have decided that I want to speak out against my aggressor and inspire others to speak out against sexual assault. Maybe I can make a difference. My friends are just helping to add fuel to the fire, which will hopefully get Vicente expelled from Markham College.

Sandro Monteblanco comes to the hotel, and we talk about my "life story," which is what I have to describe to the psychologist tomorrow.

I lie in bed contemplating my life until two in the morning attempting to calm my nerves enough so that I can fall asleep.

Peru: Sunday, August 27th, 2018

My mom went to the United States Embassy this morning. I ride to the Fiscalía with Sandro Monteblanco's junior associate or rather lawyer-in-training. We talk about traveling and various customs around the world. I want to practice my Spanish, so the junior associate and I talk about her job in Spanish.

My mom gives her interview first, and it lasts two hours. I am super enthusiastic about telling my life story, which takes around three and a half hours. The psychologist asks me questions about my friends, family, home life, boyfriends, pets, passions, substance abuse, and religion. I feel like a few of the questions are loaded questions, but I remain calm and collected.

I feel that most of the questions aren't related to the case. One of the questions is, "Do you masturbate?" What is the relevance of that question? Sandro

Monteblanco overhears it and is surprised that I am even asked that question. Regardless of my answer, would that prove anything about the case?

My mom and I don't return to the hotel until five in the evening. My mom is tired, so she goes to sleep. I get a few texts from Desiree, who calls me to talk about the rape. It seems like people are talking, which is a good thing. The more people talk, the better it is for everyone, except for my rapist of course. I want to leave Peru knowing that I made a difference, and if some people want to call me a slut or a whore and believe Vicente, they can go screw themselves because I know I'm better than that.

Peru: Tuesday, August 28th, 2018

We meet with the headmaster of Markham College because one of my Peruvian friends sent me a text yesterday explaining that the headmaster of Markham College wanted to meet with my mom, my lawyer, and me. I just want to be at home reading a book in my bed. The meeting at Markham College is awful because the headmaster says he won't take any action until the case reaches a verdict. The problem with that is that it could take years. Sure, go ahead and harbor a rapist who is a danger to every female student at Markham College.

Yesterday, Sandro Monteblanco met with a journalist from a news website, *El Popular*, and they just published an article about my case. They mentioned Jay's parents' names, and they were a little off with the dates, but no harm done because now most of Peru will know my story. Peru is corrupt, and Sandro Monteblanco thinks it's vital to involve the media. By involving the media, a spotlight is put on the case, and the chances of any unlawful bribes being paid decrease. We are trying to investigate just how powerful the rapist's family is. We suspect his family's pockets are likely deep, and his family likely has connections.

When I return to the hotel, I give two interviews in Spanish. I am uncomfortable because I am quite self-conscious when speaking in Spanish. The reporters take a lot of footage of my hands because, under Peruvian law, minors' eyes need to be covered up in any aired footage.

Then an interviewer from *El Comercio* interviews me in the hotel media room, which is this little room with bleak, white walls and a business table. The interviews all end around nine at night. I feel like a movie star but not in a good way. I have lost my sense of privacy, and it is exhausting.

Peru: Wednesday, August 29th, 2018

The news stations aired last night. Sandro Monteblanco received calls from Channel Two, Nine, and Four, and they all want to interview me! Channel

Two, Nine, and Four air on Sundays. ATV is going to air tonight, and my mom is going live. I just want us to go home.

Beto Ortiz from ATV is interviewing my mom live at ten tonight. My mom asks me if I want to fly back home alone because she has to stay to do a live interview, but I don't want to leave my mom alone here in Lima.

I give four interviews in English today. I do a lot of filming outside. I retell my story four times. I can't wait until the interviews air. The interviews are done in the hotel media room. My interviews that aired yesterday got the attention of the Peruvian Ombudsman and the Ministry of Women and Vulnerable People. Hopefully, they will keep an eye on the case.

I am upset that I am missing my grade-wide camping trip, and I still have to finish the book for school that I am supposed to read over the summer. I feel like my life is turning into a soap opera.

Peru: Thursday, August 30th, 2018

I am feeling homesick. We have an interview with Channel Five at 10:30 in the morning. Yay, I guess I have to recount the story yet again. Because the reporter thinks the hotel media room is too drab, she wants to film outdoors, so we go to a park. I speak in English, but after the interview I talk to the news reporter in Spanish. In my interview, I make a point to highlight the fact that Markham College is actively choosing to harbor a rapist.

A Markham College student sends me a text about how I am bad-mouthing the school. It's appalling that she thinks Markham College's reputation is more important than the safety of the school's students! I send the text to Sandro Monteblanco, who shares it with the news media.

I feel like a movie star, but I miss not standing out in a crowd. I miss blending in with everyone else. I feel bad for celebrities. Two park groundskeepers walk up to me and tell me that they saw me on the news last night, and they are glad that I am speaking out against sexual violence.

Two of my Peruvian friends come over, and we walk to Larcomar to eat crepes. They tell me that they are being bullied by Vicente's friends and their other classmates because they are supporting me. It's funny how millions of Peruvians support me and just the tiny little bubble of Markham College despises me for tarnishing the school's reputation.

According to Sandro Monteblanco, other private schools are starting to talk about sexual violence, including the school his children attend. Sandro Monteblanco also says that my rapist's family fired their old lawyer and hired a new, more expensive lawyer. He explains that the lawyer my rapist's family hired is the lawyer someone hires if they are found holding a gun while standing over a corpse.

Tonight, I am flying home. Thank goodness!

Los Angeles: Friday, August 31st, 2018

Last night, the rapist's family issued a press statement. In summary, their press statement said that the medical examination indicated that I wasn't raped. I can't believe that the family would label me as a liar and twist the words of a medical examiner. I am worried, but Sandro Monteblanco says he is working on it. In the medical examination, the examiner said that I had "past lesions." According to Sandro Monteblanco's experts, the word "past," when utilized in a medical examination, means that penetration occurred more than eight days prior to the exam. I took the medical examination sixteen days after the rape. The defense council alleged that since I had "past lesions," there was no way I was a virgin prior to the rape as I had stated. They claimed that since they believed I was lying about being a virgin prior to the assault, I was therefore lying about rape in general. I am so mad that the rapist's family is making me out to be a liar and a slut.

I am finally home. My dad managed to lose Tigress, my milk snake. I decide not to look for her because at some point she always shows up after escaping. As I am putting my pencil case away, I find Tigress. She had slithered into a roll of Scotch tape.

SEPTEMBER

Los Angeles: Saturday, September 1st, 2018
We get a call from Sandro Monteblanco, and he tells us we have to do some more filming via Skype that will be added to the coverage that is scheduled to air tomorrow. Sandro Monteblanco wants us to do a Skype interview, so we can explain our press statement addressing the defense council's interpretation of "past lesions." Sandro Monteblanco has learned that some news media is backing away from reporting on the story. From previous statements made by the reputable journalist Beto Ortiz, there is a great deal of pressure by the rapist's family not to air the story. That angers me. Sandro Monteblanco explains that Channel Two and Nine will still air; however, Channel Five is probably out.

Last night, I told Lola about the rape. My mom wants to call Lola's parents to check in with them, but I don't want her to.

School starts on Tuesday. Camila is super busy, and she tells me that one of our friends asked her out. He literally asks every girl out, so she denied his request.

I stay up until one in the morning because I am obsessively cleaning. I feel drained with all the Peru stuff. I don't want to continue the case. I feel like the rapist's family is throwing money right and left, and I just have to keep watching my family suffer.

Los Angeles: Sunday, September 2nd, 2018

Hopefully, I'll be home for a while. I am tired of traveling. My parents are willing to keep fighting the court case, but I feel done.

I spend the morning studying for my driving test. My sister, my mom, and I go to Chadwick to walk through my sister's classes. It's her first year of middle school. I have a class in the 800's building, in the elementary school, which is strange to me because the classroom is the same classroom I had as a third-grader. I have no idea what Chadwick is thinking by putting high school student classrooms right next to the third through sixth grade classrooms. What if the little kids hear the high schoolers cursing?

I go over to Lola's house. I love her, but I feel like she cares so much about her own problems that she struggles to focus on other people's problems.

As a family, we watch my interviews on Channel Two and Nine, and they are amazing. Only Channel Four and Five seemed to have been successfully silenced by Vicente's family. There is so much corruption in this world. A few days ago, Markham College released a press statement, which summarized that they wouldn't take action until there is a conviction. Vicente will likely be out of high school by the time all of this is over. The media loves my story, which is great. It gives me hope. I'm starting to feel a little better.

Los Angeles: Monday, September 3rd, 2018

Today is a good day in the sense that I don't hear anything about the case. Last night, I told Elliott about the rape. He seemed to handle it well. I feel like such an awful friend because I feel like I am burdening him by telling him about the rape stuff. He said he had a good summer. I missed Elliott because, even though he is technically my ex, he is still one of my closest friends.

I am starting to realize that there are some good people in the world, and I need to forgive myself. I blame myself for even going to the party in the first place.

I am nervous about my driving license test this Friday. It's going to be a good year full of self-recovery. Am I ready for life to go back to normal?

Los Angeles: Tuesday, September 4th, 2018
It's my first day of sophomore year. Most of my classes consist of people who I am not close to. Maybe I'll be able to develop some new friendships. Overall, I will make it a good year. I am not sure what I am going to do about Elliott because we don't have any classes together.

In theater class, we do this exercise where we have to hug people. I have to hug Bryan. Bryan is Elliott's cousin, and he is also part of my friend group at school. While he and I are in the same friend group, I am not super close with him, but Elliott is my best guy friend by far. Normally, I would be chill with hugging someone, but hugging Bryan triggers me. My emotions force me to swiftly leave the black box theatre, so I can cry alone in the bathroom.

Vicente got served today. His testimony is set for September 13th. So far, the case is going better than we could have hoped.

I spend most of my free time alone. It's not because I don't have friends. I am just tired of people. They take so much energy out of me. I have been too busy to think about school and my classes because my mind is occupied with thoughts about the case.

Los Angeles: Friday, September 7th, 2018
Yay, it's Friday, but I have been sick since Wednesday. My head has been hurting too much to journal, and I haven't been going to school. Wow, there have been four days of school so far this year, and I have only gone to school once. I feel bad about missing school. This isn't how I wanted this year to start out.

I found out that my parents sent Sandro Monteblanco a large check. I feel like that money is going to waste. I doubt Vicente will end up in jail because of the corruption in Peru. I feel awful. I had another nightmare last night.

Despite having a 104-degree fever, I pass my driving license test. It is easier than I expected it would be. I get marked off nine ticks, and I could miss up to fifteen. To celebrate, my mom buys me boba. The driving test is only fifteen minutes long, and it's the exact route my driving instructor had taken me on when I first learned how to drive.

I have time to talk to Gabe for an hour and a half. We play this game that I call the question game where we ask each other questions back and forth. Then Elliott calls, and we chat until midnight, which isn't smart because I'm sick. We ask each other about our summers. Wow, I missed him, and I remember why he is my best friend. He is such an amazing human!

Los Angeles: Saturday, September 8th, 2018

I'm still sick. I woke up eight times last night, and I feel like I'm dying. It's awful. My mom is convinced I have mono. We spend an hour Googling and stressing over the symptoms of mono. I've been sick for four days. We go to urgent care, and I take a strep throat and a mono test. Both tests come back negative.

My parents are disappointed in me right now. The problem with the case is that I have to tell my parents everything I did over the summer. I am supposed to be a teenager. Teenagers keep secrets. The more my parents know about the things I did, the more they are disappointed in me. There is no punishment parents can enforce that is greater than their disappointment. With the case, anything I don't share with my parents and my lawyer could leak out and negatively affect the case. For example, at the first event I went to in Peru, I kissed my rapist, which was one month prior to the rape. I have a photo of it on my phone. My lawyer turns the photo in as evidence because the rapist claimed he didn't know me prior to the night he raped me. This is just one of the many lies that my rapist has been spreading.

If there was no case and I had kept the rape to myself, I wouldn't have to expose all my secrets to my parents. I feel like everyone keeps judging me. I feel like I keep disappointing everyone I care about. How do I keep living this way?

Los Angeles: Sunday, September 9th, 2018

I still feel sick, but I am starting to get better. My fever has gone down, but my throat is getting worse. It has developed white patches that are super gross.

While I am out having coffee with my mom, she tells me that Rafe's mom is a rape survivor. I am shocked. Rafe's mom is like a second mother to me. As I am talking to my mom, tears stream down my face. If Rafe's mom was able to move on, that gives me hope that I will be able to move past it as well.

Now that I am slightly better from my illness, I am re-entering the state of being an emotional wreck. I love my friends, but I am getting vibes that they think I should be over this traumatic experience. I am realizing this is going to take me years to heal from. I don't even feel safe in my own house. I don't enjoy spending time with people. I can drive now, but I haven't yet. I am nervous about driving in a car alone. I have barely talked to Camila, and I think that's a problem. I need to talk to her soon. I wonder if she's okay.

Los Angeles: Tuesday, September 11th, 2018

I am still sick. I wake up with a 103-degree fever, but I have to go to school tomorrow, so I am going to pretend that I am feeling fine. My dad makes me breakfast, and he buys me a hamburger for lunch.

I am stressed out because the defense council has just asked Jay to testify. That worries my lawyer. Because Jay is a minor, they can't force her to testify. I hope Jay's parents insist that she doesn't testify because that would calm down my parents. Now, my rapist's family is hurting people I care about. I can't stand it. I get that there are evil people in the world, but they have no right to threaten people I care about. Being raped is one thing but watching people I care about crumble down around me is another. It's not fair. This isn't the justice I wanted.

Ever since I got back from Peru, Gabe has been texting me every single night at eight, and I am afraid that my mom will force me to cut off my contact with Gabe. I'm worried because Gabe is one of my major outlets.

Los Angeles: Thursday, September 13th, 2018

It has been two whole months since the rape. I am struggling to cope with what happened.

I have a conference with my advisor at school. I feel like she is asking probing questions, and I'm just not in a good mood. I know that it is her job to make sure her advisees are doing okay, but I am not okay, and I doubt I will be for a very long time. I sit there and smile, which is my go-to reaction when I feel like I am breaking down inside.

Vicente testified, but his lawyers convinced the prosecutor to change the location of the testimony. Sandro Monteblanco wasn't told about the change in location, so he was unable to question Vicente. One can only wonder what defendants have to do to make situations like this possible.

Sandro Monteblanco thinks at some point my mom and I will have to go back to Peru. I am convinced that the rapist's family hired a hitman, and that thought keeps me up at night. His family is dirty, so I wouldn't put anything past them.

Because I have been sick, I have been doped up on NyQuil, which enables me to just pass out. NyQuil makes it so my nightmares are less frequent, and I can sleep through the night.

I have a therapy session with my new therapist. My schedule feels so crazy. Vicente deserves to burn in hell, the deepest, hottest pits of hell.

Los Angeles: Friday, September 14th, 2018
I still haven't gone to school for an entire week because I have been sick. My throat still hurts a little, but overall, today is a good day. I'm so preoccupied thinking about the case. I feel like it's never going to go away.

My parents are prohibiting me from talking to Gabe because they don't trust anyone in Peru. I miss talking to him. My mom says I have to wait until next Tuesday when she will reconsider the ban.

Sandro Monteblanco isn't responding to my mom's texts, which is making her think the worst. Why is this world so messed up?

I babysit the girls. I have been babysitting two girls since I was in seventh grade. We invented a game based on stories of the Amazons, a tribe of female warriors in Greek mythology. The game consists of attacking each other with hand-crafted "swords" made of multiple markers stuck together. When I'm babysitting kids, all thoughts of Peru and the rape go out the window. It has been three months since I saw them last, and they remember the game we invented better than I do. I go to a park with the girls, and we watch *Zootopia* at a movie night that their elementary school is hosting.

Los Angeles: Saturday, September 15th, 2018

Some of my friends come over, and we hike down the cliff in front of my house. We eat Subway sandwiches, except for Lola, whom we tease because she has to eat pasta: she is carb-loading for a cross-country meet. Camila is picky about what she eats, so she has lunch before she comes over. Even though Camila isn't a vegan, we all tease her and call her a vegan. She doesn't mind that much. Elliott teases me constantly, but I don't mind it. I have thick skin. On the excursion, I bring my miniature schnauzer, Pepper. We attempt to swim in the tide pools, but it's too rocky. Lola, Elliott, and I discover a new route up the cliff, while the rest of the group takes the regular trail back to my house.

I am trying to figure out if I still like Elliott because it's hard to tell. He is my best friend, and I realize that with all the current emotional stress in my life, I don't have the ability to date anyone. That would complicate my life.

Los Angeles: Thursday, September 20th, 2018

I have a ton of homework, and it's all due tomorrow. When I return home from school, my mother tells me I have to rewrite an account of the rape for my new psychiatrist, and that takes about two hours. My psychiatrist is going to write a statement about my mental health and my PTSD to add to the case file. As we discuss my rape, she asks how I am doing with the anti-depressants and sleeping medication she prescribed for me a couple weeks ago.

Beto Ortiz, the news reporter who interviewed my mom live, is on his way to Los Angeles to interview me. Everything is happening so suddenly. Sandro Monteblanco calls, and we talk for two hours to prepare for the interview. I am going to have to miss yet another day of school. I am stressed out, but at least this is good news.

With all this chaos, I will be able to push back my homework until Monday.

I hate being around people. I barely eat anything, and the sleeping medication I started taking makes me dizzy every single morning. I want my life to go back to normal, with school being my number-one priority; however, right now, it feels like I am living a dual life. At least I can drive. I guess that gives me some sense of control while everything else is out of my control.

Notes for the interview in my own home:
- ◊ No revealing new information about the case
- ◊ Be compelling
- ◊ Make sure that Peru doesn't forget about the case
- ◊ No cursing
- ◊ People need to see ME

What I need to talk about
- ◊ My experience
- ◊ How I felt
- ◊ How I feel now

Phrases to highlight:
- ◊ "Some people might say I don't act like a rape victim, but there is no guidebook on how a rape victim should act."
- ◊ "I was drugged and raped at fifteen."
- ◊ "I am not going to cower in a corner."
- ◊ Use "rape, penetrate, and violate"

Los Angeles: Friday, September 21st, 2018

I wake up and take a drive to the market to buy some carrot juice and some breakfast. Eating is a struggle. I can't calm my nerves, so I end up throwing up my breakfast anyway. Sandro Monteblanco is too busy, so he can't fly up from Peru, but he sends his junior associate, who is going to spend a few days at our house. When Beto Ortiz, the news reporter, arrives, I recount my entire story again. The only difference is now Peru will see my face. Minors can't show their eyes on TV in Peru; however, if the video footage is filmed in another country, their eyes can be shown. I believe that eyes are the window into someone's soul, so it's important for Peru to see my face. I don't want this to come back to haunt me. It probably will, though.

I take a bunch of video footage walking around the house and playing with my pets. I also talk quite a bit in Spanish. It is awful, but I still have to do it. I wonder when this is going to air.

After the filming ends at four, I go to babysit the girls. The oldest one and I spend some quality time together as I try to give her age-appropriate life advice. I get home around ten at night. My entire family seems to be running on a late schedule, so we end up having family dinner with Sandro Monteblanco's junior associate from 10:15 until 11:30 at night. It is a long day.

Los Angeles: Monday, September 24th, 2018

Every year, I try to bond with my teachers. It's vital to develop good relationships with them because I'll be with them for a year. So far, the teacher I feel closest to is Rose. She has asked us to call her by her first name, which I am not used to doing. I am having a rough day, and I need to vent, so I tell Rose about what happened to me in Peru. Rose is a survivor of attempted rape. Kindred souls can find one another. I just get good vibes from her.

I have an argument with a peer, who says that she doesn't believe in the Me Too movement because she claims, "The vast majority of sexual assault victims lie, and in reality, we should be more sympathetic towards the college boys who are wrongly accused of sexual assault." I become super triggered. If only she could feel my pain and fear. The aftermath is the worst part. It never ends.

Every other news station except for Beto Ortiz's had been silenced by the prosecutor. Sandro Monteblanco explains that it is very uncommon for prosecutors to issue gag orders to media stations. It is evident that ulterior motives are at play here. Despite the prosecutor telling Beto Ortiz's boss not to air the show, Beto Ortiz airs a two-minute teaser segment. The full report is airing tomorrow. It looks pretty good to me. Hopefully, Beto Ortiz isn't fired for disobeying his boss. My rapist is testifying on October 2nd. He has six witnesses lined up. I have never met any of the witnesses formally, and many of them are Vicente's close friends.

Los Angeles: Tuesday, September 25th, 2018

All the other newspapers and media have been issued gag orders regarding my case, so none of them risked reporting the story. Beto Ortiz said that in his thirty-three years of experience, never once has he seen a prosecutor issue a gag order, and he has even reported on various corrupt presidents. The last president of Peru exiled him from the country because of his reporting, and he went to live for a while in New York. When the president left office, Beto Ortiz returned to Peru.

In response to the bullying, rather than airing a twenty-minute segment like he intended, he spends the entirety of his hour and a half showing videos of me and talking about the case. Beto Ortiz is super brave, but I don't want to be the reason he ends up being fired. Sandro Monteblanco has been working on getting three expert opinions on the psychologist's report. During my testimony in August, the defense brought in their own psychologist to "analyze my behavior" while I gave my testimony. The psychologist submitted a report explaining how I couldn't be a victim of rape because she claimed that there were eleven reasons why I didn't act like a rape victim. Well, how is a rape victim supposed to act?

My psychiatrist is one of our witnesses who reviewed the faulty report. She thinks the evil psychologist's report is bogus. I can barely focus in classes because I constantly feel anxious. I guess that is to be expected.

Because Sandro Monteblanco wasn't present while Vicente gave his testimony, the court rescheduled it for some time next week. Who knows if it's even going to happen?

Despite all this chaos, I am starting to like Elliott again.

Los Angeles: Wednesday-Friday, September 26th-28th, 2018

On Wednesday, a classmate said something that triggered me. He proclaimed, "Mackenzie, I am labeling you because you are a woman, and women are objects, so they should be labeled." He meant it as a joke, but it was offensive.

Beto Ortiz airs more of the segment about me. Thank goodness he hasn't been fired yet. I am just so tired of living a dual life. There is the Mackenzie who goes to school and does normal activities, and there is the Mackenzie who is a feminist fighting a never-ending criminal court case in Peru.

I have therapy, and I kind of feel like I'm drowning. Junior year is tough, but if I can be resilient in fighting a court case, I can put that same energy into school. I have a Spanish test, a grammar test, and a science quiz on Friday.

My therapist thinks I should journal more about my feelings so here I go…I just feel numb.

OCTOBER

Los Angeles: Tuesday, October 2nd, 2018

Guess who gave his testimony today. My rapist! Sandro Monteblanco calls to tell us about Vicente's testimony. Vicente claims that I was the aggressive one and that he took pity on me, which is why, according to him, he "had consensual sex with me." He also proclaims that I went to another party afterwards to look for more guys to have sex with. When actually, I passed out as soon as I returned to my host's house. Keep in mind I was still doped up on the drug he gave me. Sandro Monteblanco reports that during Vicente's testimony, Vicente was sweating, red-faced, and kept looking nervously at his lawyer periodically. That makes me laugh.

I never want to have sex. How the hell is it supposed to feel good? I don't think other people understand the magnitude of how a sexual assault affects someone's life.

Los Angeles: Thursday, October 11th, 2018

Sandro Monteblanco has barely contacted me. The case comes before all else, and if I have to fly down to Peru, I will do it right this second. No questions asked.

I call Elliott to ask him to the Homecoming dance because it's a girls-ask-guys dance. I have to meet with my parents at Good Stuff to discuss the case, so I can't ask Elliott in person. I call him partly because I don't want anyone to ask him first and partly because I never know when I will or will not be at school. He tells me to ask him in person, not over the phone, but I have a lot going on right now. I am barely at school. I honestly can't say for certain that I will be at school tomorrow. What if something case related comes up? I have so much case stuff to worry about. After the call, I spend an hour making him a poster that basically sums up all of our inside jokes.

Gabe reads a bedtime story to me in Spanish. It's funny because Gabe is such a special person, but he doesn't realize it, and I think that is why I admire him to the extent that I do.

Los Angeles: Friday, October 12th, 2018

At school, I ask Elliott to walk with me to my car. I hope that he will say yes to my Homecoming ask. Elliott seems off. I know he is super busy with football right now, but judging from his demeanor, I think something else is wrong. I ask him to Homecoming, and he says yes. I feel content. Even though I ask Elliott to Homecoming, he seems sad. I hope he's okay. I ask him how he's doing, and he just says okay. I don't want to pry, so I decide to just leave it at that. I'm sure that he will talk to me about what's bugging him eventually.

Los Angeles: Saturday, October 13th, 2018

I'm sick again. I don't have a weak immune system, but my life has been stressful. It's all good because I am able to accomplish a tremendous amount of work at home.

I FaceTime Elliott and pour my heart out. I ask him if he likes me, but he keeps dodging that question. That means he likes me, right? Because if he doesn't, I think he would tell me he doesn't. Thinking about Elliott is the only time I can get myself to stop thinking about the case. It has become my way out, and I think that has increased my feelings for him. I hope, regardless of his feelings or lack of feelings towards me, that he can be honest with me. That's all I ask.

I find out that Bryan kissed Lola when they were at my house last weekend. Good for them, I guess. I'm surprised it took a week for Lola to tell me. She tends to tell me stuff right away. How did I miss that? I guess I was just too busy paying attention to Elliott.

It has been three months since the rape, and I have realized that all of this has been my own fault. I believe in karma. Because I was raped, I had to have done something that deserved it in the past. I'm a demon-child, and I am so awful to my parents. I push away everyone who cares about me. No wonder all my friends from eighth grade ditched me my freshman year. In conclusion, I don't deserve to be on this earth. I got what was coming to me. I am destroying my family members' lives. My siblings deserve a better older sister. My parents deserve a nicer child. Camila deserves a better friend.

Los Angeles: Sunday, October 14th, 2018

Elliott hasn't returned my calls or texts about my costume ideas for Homecoming for about a week. Part of me thinks he is ignoring me. We passed each other at school yesterday, and he didn't say hi to me. I have to talk to Elliott about Homecoming costume ideas. Elliott's latest idea is that we should wear "very fake news" t-shirts. The phrase "very fake news" is one of Donald Trump's favorite insults for media platforms that say anything negative about him.

I asked my mom about Elliott's costume idea. My mom tells me that if I wear a shirt with that phrase, she will disown me. Then she breaks down crying on the floor because she connects the shirt to Donald Trump, and she realizes that we have an alleged sexual assault offender as president, which reminds her of how I was raped. This is just one more example of my family breaking down around me.

No one understands the extent I have suffered. Every time my mom breaks down crying, I know I can't cry or allow her to see I am upset because I have to be the one in the family who is strong. I also don't know what to do when she's upset. I just sit down on the floor with her while she cries. I just feel numb. The best way to get through it is to just block it out.

Elliott might still be a little bit hurt after hearing the details of my summer. He can't even have a serious conversation with me. I need the friend that I had in Elliott. I need stable people in my life, but when they don't ever say hi in the hallways at school, are they important to me? He should at least have some compassion. But hey, what do I know? I'm just damaged goods anyway.

Los Angeles: Friday, October 19th, 2018

Elliott tells me that his idea of wearing "very fake news" shirts was a joke. I took it literally. If only he knew the chaos it caused in my house.

I argue with my math teacher about standards-based grading, which is a new, awful, mandatory grading system at my school. Nowadays, any true argument I have just results in me breaking down and crying; therefore, I break down and start crying. I end up skipping Spanish because I need to vent, and my math teacher is free the next period. I tell her about the rape.

Right after, the dean of students and I go for a walk around campus as I calm down. The dean of students is amazing. She always provides me with much-needed support. My parents told my school about the rape at the beginning of the year. My parents want to make sure I have a strong support system at school in case I become triggered.

Normally, I drive to school, but this morning my mom took away my car privileges because I wasn't in the car right at 7:20 in the morning, per rules my brother invented and my parents enforce. I try to call my parents to pick me up. My mom is sleeping, and my dad is running errands, so he can't pick me up until later in the afternoon.

I end up skipping theater class, and Bryan texts me right before class and asks why I am not there. I tell him I am upset, and he tells the theater teacher that he has to use the bathroom. He walks to where I am. The dean of students tells him he can stay with me. Bryan helps me feel better, and pretty soon we are talking and laughing on the main lawn; however, the theater teacher sees the two of us right after class, and he drags us to the black box theatre. He starts yelling at Bryan and me. Our other theater teacher, meanwhile, is sitting in a chair, hugging a teddy bear, and staring at his shoes.

I have already had a rough day, and I am past the point of being upset. I am angry because now I am getting Bryan, who is trying to be a good friend to me, in trouble. So, in a fit of angry tears, I stare my theater teacher straight in the eyes and exclaim, "This summer I was drugged and raped!" My theater teacher retorts, "I didn't need to know that." Hell yes, he did.

Then he marches us to the dean's office. Unfortunately, it is during a break, so a bunch of other students watch us as we walk to the dean's office. After speaking with my theater teacher, the dean tells me that it isn't my fault or Bryan's fault.

Los Angeles: Saturday, October 20th, 2018
I decide that I will be diplomatic and clear stuff up with my theater teacher via email. I send him an email telling him that nothing was his fault, and that I understand why he reacted the way he did. He responds a minute later, and we decide to start a fresh. Of course, he feels guilty for his actions. I don't think he deserves to stew in his feelings of guilt. He's human, and we all make mistakes.

I attend the Homecoming football game. Then I drive to Camila's house to get ready for the dance. Elliott and I decided to go to the dance as Rick and Morty from the TV show *Rick and Morty*. I choose to be Rick. I am one of the least sluttily dressed people at the pre-party. What is it with high school girls flaunting their bodies? I spend most of the time hanging with Bryan and Camila because Elliott is ignoring me. I bring my own water bottle to the party, and I refuse to refill it anywhere but the sink. Bryan picks up on my PTSD-triggered actions and asks me if I am okay. I really appreciate that.

One of my friends tells me that Elliott is mad at me about something, but I don't know what because Elliott won't tell me. Elliott and I talk for about twenty minutes. I tell him that I still like him, and he tells me he doesn't like me. I am so embarrassed. Maybe he is just busy with football or something. I ask him if he's mad at me, and he tells me he isn't. I'm not sure I believe him because of the way he's acting towards me. He acts dismissive, and he responds to my questions by saying good, okay, or yeah. I should just be done with him. I feel like he doesn't even care about our friendship anymore.

Los Angeles: Monday, October 22nd, 2018
I have a Spanish test today, and in the simulated conversation part of the test, the name of the person

speaking is the name of my rapist. It's one thing when I say that name in context to what happened to me but seeing that infiltrate my school life, shakes me. I leave that class triggered with anger and disbelief. I call my mom, and she tries to help me calm down over the phone.

At the end of the day, I ask for a new Spanish test, and my Spanish teacher gives me another one. Thank goodness I don't have to tell her everything that has happened to me. I have already told three of my five core teachers. There seems to be a sense of understanding without verbal communication between my Spanish teacher and me.

After dinner, I drive to the gas station because my car is nearly out of gas. After filling up my tank, I pull into a parking spot, so I can buy a Slurpee. As I am backing out of the parking spot, I accidently run into a truck that is filling up on gas behind me. The truck driver is inside his truck, so I pull back into the parking spot. The man walks out of his truck and over to my window. He asks, "What are we going to do about this?"

"You can have it checked by a mechanic and text me three cost estimates," I reply.

"Are you a student?"

"Yes, I'm in high school."

"I don't want your money." He walks back into his truck and drives away.

Los Angeles: Tuesday, October 30th, 2018

I am having a normal boring school day up until seventh period when I meet with my math teacher to discuss how she graded my test because I despise standards-based grading with a passion. After that meeting, I end up crying, as usual. I don't like arguing with people.

I have therapy, which is okay, I guess. I learn some new coping mechanisms. I want to make a scrapbook filled with the various coping mechanisms that I am learning in order to be better equipped to deal with my anger. That way, when I am upset, I can flip through the pages to find a suitable coping mechanism to utilize.

Bryan and I FaceTime in order to figure out what we are going to do for Halloween. Elliott is making plans, but it's not like he will invite me. Usually, I can ignore people when they act like that, like my younger siblings, but not tonight. I just can't. I hang up the phone and chuck a pumpkin at the floor. I have no idea where all this anger is coming from. It's not normal. Bryan tries to call me back four times, but I am too riled up to want to talk to him. He is trying to be a good friend, but his cousin is acting like such an ass. I don't know what to do about it. I hope this anger goes away. I even yell at my mom for no apparent reason. My anger is all-consuming. and I think it would be best if I lock myself in my room because I am mad at the world.

NOVEMBER

Los Angeles: Tuesday, November 6th, 2018
Tomorrow is the last day to turn in evidence to the prosecutor, and my lawyer just caught wind of something that could damage our case. Desiree, the exchange student from Jordan, was at the party when I was raped. She texted me two days after the party and said that Vicente had told a bunch of people that I had sex with him. This was before I had put together what happened that night. I didn't know how to respond because I was scared, so I told her that I gave him a blowjob just to stop the conversation. I wasn't going to just come out and say that he raped me. I thought Desiree was a friend, but she forwarded screen shots of the WhatsApp conversation to some

lady who is friends with my rapist's mother. The defense submitted the WhatsApp conversation between Desiree and the lady as evidence. The WhatsApp conversation is interesting because there is a point where the lady tells Desiree that if she can dig up dirt on me, then she will purchase a trip to Cuzco for Desiree. This demonstrates a clear case of witness tampering punishable by law. If Vicente walks free because of this, I will be beyond angry. There are some very bad people in this world.

Some advice for anyone dealing with court cases: just be upfront about everything. I didn't tell my lawyer about these messages—not on purpose; I genuinely forgot—and then it came back to bite me in the butt. Everything comes out in time.

I thought Desiree was my friend. We told each other everything, and I helped her when she needed someone who could speak Spanish. I should have realized that she wasn't a good person in the five weeks that I spent with her, and this is why I am never trusting anyone right off the bat again.

Los Angeles: Thursday, November 8th, 2018

The conversation between Desiree and the friend of the rapist's mother started back in August, even before Desiree called me to express her condolences about the rape. She called me to tell me she was so sorry for what happened just so she could get information out of me. Thankfully, I am a pretty closed-off person, and Sandro Monteblanco had warned me not to tell anyone anything about the case, so she wasn't able to get much information from me. She is such an awful person. Desiree spent months calling and texting this lady. There are around thirty pages of WhatsApp messages between those two from August to November. She even sent photos of me to the lady from the night of the rape, although they weren't actual photos of me because I was off being raped. She sent the lady photos of a girl who kind of looked like me, who was also at the party.

It's funny because Desiree spent five weeks getting to know me. She had to have known the photos she sent weren't of me. I can't believe that my so-called friend would betray me. Desiree said in the WhatsApp messages to the lady, and I quote, "If these photos help Vicente, anyone can see them. I would be happy to tell you anything."

Los Angeles: Thursday, November 15th, 2018
My day is going well until my mom calls me and tells me to come home early from school because we have to Skype some news reporters from Peru.

The prosecutor told the attorney that she will have a verdict by Friday. Sandro Monteblanco says that he thinks she is leaning towards our side. My mom says that because we will probably continue and take this case to court, we are going back to Peru during Thanksgiving break. We are going to do more interviews with Beto Ortiz, and this time I get to go live because everyone has already seen my face in the video footage taken at my house.

I receive a text from Camila saying that she overheard some Chadwick students talking about my case. These students weren't supposed to know about my case. Somehow, a senior at Chadwick, who had gone to Markham College the summer before I went, heard about the rape from some students at Markham College. I knew the senior would eventually find out because he visited Peru and studied at Markham College last year, and he was in the same graduating class that I was in. At Markham College, I was moved up two grades, so I could be in the same grade as my host sister. What annoys me is that the senior told Jasmine, my ex-best friend from middle school, who then told one of the boys notorious for spreading gossip at my school.

In anger, I drive to Jasmine's house to confront her. She apologizes and promises me that she hasn't told anyone else. I call the boy she told, and he confirms that she told him.

My mom and I show up at the senior's house. Unfortunately, the senior isn't home so instead my mom and I have a nice little chat with his father. We ask the senior's father to convince his son to stop talking about me. I know nothing about this senior as a person, but I am annoyed that he is talking to people in my grade about it, especially Jasmine who in my opinion is a terrible person.

Case-wise, Sandro Monteblanco tells my mom that the rapist's father has asked my host dad from Peru to have a meeting with him and the family at whose house the party took place. My host dad told Sandro Monteblanco about the request, so I'm not sure what's going to happen. I pray that my host dad doesn't turn his back on us, but I don't trust anyone right now.

Los Angeles: Friday, November 16th, 2018

I love animals, and someday I want to be a vet. I have two snakes, two geckos, a cat, a dog, and some fish. Last night, I went to the reptile store to buy a baby rat and a baby mouse for my snakes; however, I didn't tell my dad that I was buying reptile food, so we accidentally both bought snake food. My larger snake ate her rat and the second baby mouse, but she seemed full, so I decided to keep one of the baby rats to feed her later. I bought kitten formula because baby rats need to be fed diluted kitten formula every two hours.

I fall in love with the baby rat, and I name him Peanut because he is the size of a peanut. He is tiny, and his eyes are not even open yet. A fun fact is that baby rats can't urinate on their own. Their mothers have to stimulate urine flow manually, so after every meal I have to make sure my little Peanut pees and gets a warm bath. Because he has to be fed every two hours, I take him to school with me in a little cardboard box with cotton balls and a heating pad since baby rats can't produce their own body heat. My teachers have mixed reactions. I had forgotten that it is parent-teacher conferences day, so in every class with my teachers, my parents get to hear about the baby rat. Surprisingly, I don't get in trouble for bringing the rat to school, and the majority of the teachers like having the baby rat around.

Los Angeles: Saturday, November 17th, 2018

I find a friend to take care of Peanut while I am in Peru. It's been hard waking up every two hours to feed and help my baby rat urinate. I have to acknowledge that there's a chance Peanut could pass away while I am gone because he looks too skinny. In the hopes of fattening him up, I have started adding peanut butter to every other kitten milk dilution I give to him.

I decide to spend the day with my friends. We all go bowling. Then we chill in a mattress shop. My mom picks up everyone to drive them to the Riviera, and I drive myself. I can't drive my friends yet. In the state of California, minors have to have a license for a year before they can drive with passengers under the age of twenty-five. We eat Mexican food and walk to James' house. James is a close school friend of mine. My friends live in the South Bay, ranging from Manhattan Beach to Palos Verdes. It takes around forty minutes to drive from my house, in Palos Verdes, to my friends' houses in Manhattan Beach; therefore, James' house in Redondo Beach is the ideal halfway meeting place.

We hang out at the beach for a few hours and have a bean-bag battle. I have terrible aim, and one of the bean bags I throw accidently hits Elliott in the balls. I feel pretty bad afterwards. We start talking about what girls could relate the pain to. During this conversation, I start having flashbacks of the rapist shoving his dick down my throat, so I curl up in a ball on the sand and refuse to talk to anyone.

Bryan notices my change in demeanor, and he tries to comfort me. Then Elliott exclaims, "Bryan, it looks like you raped her." That quote not only makes me more upset, but it also ignites anger inside of me. Elliott knows that I was raped, and he still would make a rape joke. Also, is that what a rape victim looks like, curled up in a ball like that? Because I sure as hell didn't look like that while I was giving my testimony or giving interviews to the Peruvian media. There is no guidebook to how a rape victim should act. Why am I calling myself a victim? I hate that word. I'm going to refer to myself as a survivor because that's what I am. I have been through hell and back, yet he still has the audacity to make that joke.

I walk away from the group, and Camila runs to catch up with me. We walk on the beach until I calm down. When we return to the group, the conversation resumes like normal.

Los Angeles: Monday, November 19th, 2018

I'd made plans to wake up at nine, but my mom frantically wakes me up at seven. She is freaking out because the United States Embassy sent an agent to the prosecutor's office, and the prosecutor was having a secret meeting with Vicente's family. According to standard procedure, any meeting with the prosecutor has to be logged and the other side must be informed; however, my lawyers weren't informed. When my lawyers called the prosecutor out on her actions, she denied us a meeting. Very suspicious.

My mom makes me write a letter to the prosecutor, talking about justice and how important the case is to me. She faxes it over to Sandro Monteblanco. I hope that goes well. This case is such an emotional roller coaster, not just for me, but also for my entire family.

I hang out with my friends in Manhattan Beach. Elliott and I get into an argument about how the

United States has a male-orientated mindset. He argues that the United States doesn't. I claim that we have a president who has thirteen cases of sexual assault filed against him, so what message does that send to the rest of America?

Los Angeles → Peru: Tuesday, November 20th, 2018

My mom isn't in the best mood, and she doesn't tell me why until we are driving to the airport. It turns out that my host dad didn't go to the prosecutor like he told us he would. Sandro Monteblanco theorizes that my host dad's abandonment of his promise could likely be because his wife is friends with the rapist's mother. So, my host parents have betrayed me and my family.

Now, my parents are mad at my host dad, and they want to sue him. That's going to affect my relationship with Gabe. I am going to be so close to him tomorrow, yet I promise my parents that I won't talk to him. I have been banned from talking to him because his dad went back on his word. Up until the ban, Gabe has texted me every night at eight without fail since mid-August. I feel like, without texting him, I have lost a significant outlet. My parents also won't allow me to see any of my friends in Peru.

Just as the stewardesses are giving the safety speech, my mom and I receive a voice message from

Sandro Monteblanco saying that the prosecutor denied our case. It comes out of the blue. The prosecutor claims we don't have enough evidence despite our nearly 700 pages of various documents. Sandro Monteblanco says this is the first time he has had a case dropped during this stage of the investigation. There is no way to walk off this plane now. Unless my mom or I fake a heart attack or something, we are destined for Peru.

Peru: Wednesday, November 21st, 2018

My mom and I meet Sandro Monteblanco at our hotel, and we make the decision to appeal the case and continue fighting for justice. We are all convinced that the prosecutor may have been persuaded to dismiss our case. Her report summed up the rapist's lawyers' arguments. She even stated that because I had no physical markings on my body and I was partly conscious during the rape, it had to have been consensual. Her verdict sends the message that rapists should feel free to rape as many women as they want as long as they don't beat them first, and they should drug them with ketamine to keep them conscious but simultaneously immobile because as long as they are conscious it's consensual. I can't believe that a woman, a mother, would propagate that horrendous message. This society is messed up.

I spend the day giving interviews. We videotape in front of the house where the party took place, Markham College's gates, Jay's house, the Fiscalía, and in the park to wrap up the filming. At Markham College, Sandro Monteblanco asks a group of painters if he can park in the house's driveway, which is right across the street from Markham College. The painters ask if I am Mackenzie. I wonder what gave it away—maybe the cameras. Sandro Monteblanco confirms my identity, and they say they would be happy to have us park there. Now I know what it's like to be famous. As much as I like having people know my name, I wouldn't like to be famous like this back in Los Angeles.

In the evening, Beto Ortiz spends around forty minutes talking about me on air, and then he rips apart the rapist's lawyer. It is fascinating to watch. Beto Ortiz asks Vicente's lawyer, "If a minor comes forward with charges of sexual assault, should people believe her?" The lawyer flat-out says no. Well, 92% - 98% of reported sexual assaults are true, so…

Peru: Thursday, November 22nd, 2018

Happy Thanksgiving, America. Yay, I get to spend Thanksgiving in a foreign country without my entire immediate family.

Despite being stressed with case stuff, I summon my inner productivity and finish all of my take-home

AP Spanish tests, and I work on my history essay and English essay in the hotel room. Sometimes it's good to compartmentalize thoughts about the case, to focus on schoolwork.

Sandro Monteblanco comes to our hotel to talk about the show tonight. We evaluate the reasons the prosecutor dismissed my case.

1) The toxicology evaluation: While it stated there were no drugs in my system, that could very well be the case given that I took the toxicology exam sixteen days after the rape, which only consisted of a urine test. We theorize Vicente drugged me with ketamine, which can no longer be detected in urine after eleven days. So, timing-wise, it would have been out of my system by the time I took the toxicology evaluation. We have the founder of the first toxicology school in all of Latin America and Spain as one of our witnesses, who corroborated the fact that by the time I had taken the toxicology evaluation, the ketamine I was drugged with would have been out of my system.

2) The so-called witness, also known as one of Vicente's friends who likely didn't even see me at the party, claimed I didn't look "normal" for a rape victim. Should I have run out of the room naked and screaming that I had just been raped? Oh, right, I

couldn't run or scream. What should a "normal" rape victim look like anyway?

3) After an hour and fifteen minutes, if I had been drugged, how was I able to walk out of the party? I have the flight-or-fight phenomenon to explain that. I knew I had to leave the dangerous situation as soon as possible. According to the toxicologist, it is also possible that the rapist gave me a small dosage of ketamine that would have worn off in an hour and fifteen minutes.

4) The prosecutor implied that I was unconscious; therefore, I couldn't know that I had been raped. Never once in my testimony or in any of my interviews did I say that I was unconscious. I was conscious but incapacitated, so I was unable to reach my phone to call for help.

5) In her notes, the prosecutor claimed I couldn't have been drugged because I remembered too much. During my testimony, I was asked to remember as much as I could, and most of those memories were of excruciating pain. How much is a rape victim drugged supposed to remember?

I love how the truth remains constant. All four of the witnesses, all of whom were Vicente's friends, had different and contradicting testimonies. How is it that the varying testimonies were more credible than the consistent account of the survivor and legal experts opinions?

Peru: Friday, November 23rd, 2018

I spend most of the day chilling at the hotel being productive. I finish up my English essay. My mom and I leave the hotel to get crepes, which is the first time we have left the hotel this trip without being escorted by Sandro Monteblanco.

Sandro Monteblanco comes over in the evening to discuss the updates for the case. We have a lot of public support because we managed to highlight the corruption in Peru's legal system. Sandro Monteblanco attempts to explain to me the legal hierarchy, and I kind of understand it. There are two stages of prosecution to determine whether or not the case will go to court. We filed an appeal, so the case is moving to the superior prosecutor. There are only seven superior prosecutors in Lima. If the superior prosecutor dismisses the case, it won't go to court, and then we will be done. Sandro Monteblanco turned in our appeal, and an hour later it had already been admitted into process. Sandro Monteblanco explains that the admission process usually takes a month, but our case had been admitted and received in under an hour. I guess all the media coverage is quite beneficial. The case is already a thousand pages long.

One of Beto Ortiz's film crew members compared me to Donald Trump because of my fiery temper. I think it was supposed to be a compliment, but given the current situation in the United States, it's hard to say.

Sandro Monteblanco is convinced that the prosecutor had most likely decided to dismiss the case from the very beginning, and he also believes that the family who had the party is helping fund the lawyer for Vicente. I am not just fighting a family at this point; I am fighting a community of powerful people.

Up until today, the public didn't know the name of my rapist, but on live TV, I slipped and said his name. At least people know his name now. My parents will continue fighting for me. I love them to the ends of the universe, which is constantly expanding, so my love is never-ending.

I made Gabe a little pom-pom crab because it represents one of our inside jokes. I meet him at the hotel, and we talk for two hours. I admit to him that I like him, and he kisses me. Many of the guys I have kissed I haven't had prior feelings for, so this kiss feels different. In a good way. Gabe is nineteen, but that's not that much older than me, right? I'm sixteen. I have learned that when a guy says he cares about a girl, it means he likes her. Saying "I care about you" is code for "I have feelings for you." The issue is that, like Romeo and Juliet, we can't be lovers because his parents betrayed me, so my parents demanded that I cut all ties with him and his family. My logical mind is turned off, and somehow, we come to the conclusion that we should date.

Los Angeles: Sunday, November 25th, 2018

My mom gives me an ultimatum. She flat-out tells me, "Mackenzie, you have to choose Gabe or the case." I prioritize the case because throwing a rapist behind bars and motivating others to speak out against their aggressors is infinitely more important than my relationship with Gabe. I have to sacrifice my desires for the good of others, and the sooner I can move on the better. Plus, there are a thousand miles between us anyway. I am still young, so I am sure I will find someone else later in life. I promise my parents that I won't talk to him, but I don't know if I can keep that promise because Gabe is my biggest outlet.

Los Angeles: Tuesday, November 27th, 2018

I am just realizing how hellish this week is. I have two essays to work on, AP Spanish testing, a math test, and a grammar test. But there is some good news. Peanut, my rat, is alive. I picked him up from my friend's house, and he looks fatter. I am glad his diet of peanut butter appears to have helped him gain some fat. He is good at distracting me from my chaotic life. I know this sounds like weird advice, but if you're trying to deal with PTSD, you should get a rat. On the plus side, they take up less time than dogs and cats, and they can be super lovable.

I go to my balcony to call Gabe and to talk about life. Our conversation ends with my dad shutting off the Wi-Fi because he is thinks I am up too late. He doesn't know who I am talking to—if he did, I would be in so much trouble.

Los Angeles: Wednesday, November 28th, 2018

My mom doesn't talk to me all morning because she's upset with me, probably because of how late I stayed up last night. I am four minutes late, so my mom says she will drive us to school. I get upset, so I get out of the car and walk away. I am too upset to go to school. The Wi-Fi is off because my dad shut it off last night to punish me. My mom leaves to take my siblings to school, and I haven't seen my dad all morning. I assume he isn't home because he rarely sleeps in.

I want to get some work done, but I can't because my parents have also shut off my cell service. They do that when they are really mad at me. I walk over to a neighbor's house to use her Wi-Fi. I order an Uber to take me to the library, so I can work on homework. Neither of my parents are answering their cell phones, so I just leave to go to the library. The library is closed, so I go to Starbucks.

About two hours later, my mom texts me to tell me that she is going to call the police because with my cellular off, she can't track where I am. Not my problem. My parents shut it off in the first place. I slowly make my way back home. When I return, a policeman is sitting at my kitchen table. We have a nice little chat about how I should always tell my parents where I am. I tell him that they would have known had they not turned off my cell service, and I'm such a studious student that I had to go somewhere with Wi-Fi to get my schoolwork done. He doesn't know what to say to me after that, so he leaves.

I walk upstairs still mad and frustrated and use a little pocketknife to slice a cross symbol on my wrist. Partly to get back at my parents. It doesn't hurt whatsoever, and it actually makes me feel a lot better. I have never cut myself before, but it truly helps calm me down.

I attempt to explain to my family therapist why I am upset with all the rules my parents have been enforcing lately. Ever since the rape, I feel like my mother has become a helicopter parent. My mom argues that I am not taking care of my health because I stay up too late talking to people over FaceTime. She deems I need "more structure." Every time my parents impose a rule, I feel an added layer of stress just engulf me. Their new rules are smothering me.

Los Angeles: Thursday, November 29th, 2018

I stay home from school again. I don't enjoy being at school right now. I like all my teachers and close friends, but I am not a fan of the environment. I just feel like isolating myself from people. I can be more productive working by myself anyway. I wonder if my desire to withdraw is caused by my PTSD?

I have to take a math test and a Spanish test. I pick up the tests from school and take them at home. I open up to my parents and tell them that I am still in contact with Gabe. They tell me that I have until Friday to stop talking to him, or they will stop funding the case. I also tell them that I cut myself, but because they are so mad at me for the Gabe stuff, the fact that I cut myself goes over both of their heads.

I call Gabe, and we talk about the normal stuff: plans for the future, why we like each other, and our inside jokes. Gabe gives me a list of reasons why he loves me. I hang up the phone and start crying.

My parents are upset with the Gabe thing, but they haven't mentioned the cutting. I think they forgot about it. No matter. I will keep it in my tool kit as a coping mechanism for dealing with extreme emotions. It helps.

Los Angeles: Friday, November 30th, 2018

I did it. I blocked Gabe on Instagram, WhatsApp, and my contacts. That was one of the hardest things I have ever done. He means so much to me, and he is my outlet. I can talk to him about anything and he won't judge me. What am I supposed to do without my outlet? Who am I supposed to talk to? Clearly, not my parents. Their ultimatum put a dent the size of the Mariana Trench in our relationship. I just have to put all thoughts of Gabe in that little box in the depths of my brain in order to forget about him. The case has to take precedence over any feelings I have towards Gabe. I hope he understands.

DECEMBER

The rift between me and my mom has grown. I have blocked and ended all communication with Gabe, and I just feel empty.

I have lunch with my dad at my favorite restaurant. Then we head over to family therapy. Like normal, I yell at my parents, and my mom cries. I tell her that I wish I had never told her about the rape because of the devastating impact it has had on my family. She claims I always say that phrase when I want to stop the conversation, but I truly believe that. I wish I had kept it bottled up inside because then only I would be suffering, rather than my entire family. I thought therapy was a time for people to release their feelings and talk about them, but how can I do that when my mom doesn't even accept or shows little empathy for my feelings? I feel like I have to be the strong figure in my family. My mom feels like I have shut her out of my life.

Because of the trial, it feels like my entire personal life has been shared with the world. I feel like I am grasping at straws to retain even a tiny bit of privacy. My life is completely exposed to my lawyer, my parents, and the Peruvian media. I hate it. My mom is hovering over me because she is afraid that I will collapse under the pressure, but it's evident that she is the one breaking down. With her overprotectiveness, I have no freedom to be myself. I feel like I have to rebel to gain a minuscule amount of control and a sense of stability. I understand that parents should have authority over their kids. I respect my parents, but I yearn for control because for so long many aspects of my life have been out of my control.

Los Angeles: Wednesday, December 12th, 2018
I wait at school until five because I have to drive my siblings home. In my free time, I have this conversation with one of my guy friends. He says there is only one thing that he doesn't want to tell me about himself, which makes me curious. Why would someone say they have a secret and then not want to share it? Part of me believes that he wants to share it with someone. I instantly pick up on vibes that it could be

a sexual assault. I don't know how to explain how I know, but I just do. I tell him that I was raped, and he tells me that he had been raped orally when he was nine. He explains how he hasn't told anyone at our school or even his parents. Even though he is a friend of mine, I don't know him too well, and I am happy that he confides in me.

It has been five months since the rape, and I am nowhere near getting over it. If he was raped six years ago and still hasn't recovered, I am in for a long ride. He still has nightmares to this day. I am so screwed.

Los Angeles: Friday, December 14th, 2018

I think that there is something wrong with me. I want to say the devil lives inside me, but that would imply that I don't take responsibility for my actions.

I yell at my parents for refusing to let me buy another rat. I read this scientific study explaining that rats are very social creatures. If they don't have a friend, they can become depressed and start self-harming. I don't want Peanut to become depressed.

Last night I cut myself again. I was super upset with my parents, but it helped me calm down. Am I depressed? I know I have PTSD, as many trauma victims do, but I don't want to kill myself or anything. I have to make an impact on the world in terms of fighting against sexual assault. What is wrong with me? Also, I can't stop physically shaking.

I no longer have Gabe as an outlet, and now my internal thoughts are eating me up. I have no one to talk to. I am upset with my parents because they won't let me get another rat. I am taking a math test early so that I don't have to go to school on Thursday or Friday. I will have a couple of extra days of Christmas break.

I go to family therapy where I attempt to convince my parents for a complete hour that we should get a second rat. My dad shows up with a bag, and I think that he has surprised me with a rat, but he bought a mirror. My dad's rationale is that if Peanut looks in a mirror, his reflection will keep him company. I acknowledge that my dad is trying to be nice, but his actions sting stronger than any words. I end up crying and feeling miserable.

Los Angeles: Thursday, December 20th, 2018

All the drama starts when a Chadwick friend FaceTimes me in tears because she overheard two girls talking about the rape in the bathroom at a water polo game. I had told one of the girls. The other girl had been one of my close friends in middle school, but I'd disassociated myself from that friend group at the start of my freshman year. The girl I didn't tell is a notorious gossip. I didn't want her to ever find out what happened to me because she would spread it around. One of the issues with going to a small school is that everyone knows practically everything about everyone. I am not ready for my entire grade to find out about the rape.

I FaceTime the gossipy girl and ask how she found out. She tells me my whole ex-group of middle-school friends know about the rape because of Jasmine. Back in November, I went to Jasmine's house to ask her if she had told anyone that I was raped, and she promised me she had only told one boy. The gossipy girl tells me that Jasmine told her back in September that I was raped. Apparently, Jasmine was starting to lose her friends back in September. In an effort to retain her popularity status, she told the whole friend group about my rape to try to seem cool for knowing that information. She used my rape to try to weasel her way back into the friend group's inner circle. Frankly, walking away from that friend group freshman year was one of the smartest decisions I have ever made.

I am already angry. Then my mom blindsides me. According to her, I've lost my license for six months.

On Tuesday, I had a Sustainability Council meeting at the council leader's house. One of the seniors on the council who was going to drive one of the sophomore council members back to Chadwick, asked me to drive the sophomore instead because she wanted to go and get lunch, and the sophomore had to return to campus before dismissal. My parents allow me to drive other people as long as they know about it in advance. Because the turnaround time was so quick, I forgot to ask for permission.

I have been so distracted with life that I forgot to tell my mom. After my mom finishes yelling at me, I go upstairs and cut myself, but my little pocketknife slips, and I pass out because I cut too deep. When I regain my senses, my mom is shaking me, and my dad makes me sit up. My mom calls 911 and tells them that her daughter has tried to commit suicide, but that wasn't what I intended at all. I just needed to calm myself down because I have had a rough day.

Written in Del Amo Hospital:
December 21st-22nd, 2018

The first time I cut myself, my parents knew but took no notice of it whatsoever because they were so wrapped up with the Gabe stuff. It's not that I wanted to hurt myself, I just wanted to calm myself down. Anyway, I pass out on my bathroom floor, and then my mom calls the police, who come with the fire department and an ambulance.

I guess my parents thought I was trying to commit suicide, but if they would just listen to me, they would know that I'm not suicidal. The people here tell me that I have to stay for at least seventy-two hours. I ride to the hospital in an ambulance, and they keep me there for five hours. My blood pressure is checked at least five times. Why do they have to do that over and over again?

My mom stays with me for a while, and they put this depressed girl next to me, and she keeps cursing. When I try to fall asleep, I can't.

Think about it. A fifteen-year-old was raped, she is told she has depression, and ends up in a psychiatric ward. At the end of this, I will have a ton of new depressed friends.

I am strapped down to a gurney, which convinces me that I am crazy. I can't move. It is about five in the morning, and I pass out because I have sleeping medication in my system. I don't remember too much after that because I was groggy. This lady does a strip-search, but because I am doped up on sleeping pills, I nearly fall over. Once again, my body is just open for the world to see and use at its disposal.

Then they lock me in this dark room. I remember the lock clicking shut. The next morning, I realize that there are five other girls in the room with me. I am upset because they wouldn't let me bring in any of my acne medication. Great, now I'm going to have to deal with that too, and the only hairbrush that I am given is a tiny one.

My dad is convinced that I am a spoiled brat. My life would have been amazing had I not gone to that party and been raped. If I'm a spoiled brat, maybe I deserve to be locked in a psychiatric ward. This place scares me. Every waking second, I am reminded of what Vicente did to me. The problem is that I have too much time to think, and that's when my demons haunt me the most. I'm going to talk about my sixty-four hours through the other girls I met.

Dub

During my first breakfast, I sat next to Dub. She seemed like an outcast, but she was friendly and explained the rules to me. First, she told me that we have to lie about how much food we eat. A floor nurse would ask us what percentage of our food we had eaten, and the doctors wouldn't let us leave unless we were eating, so all the girls would lie, either because they were bulimic or because the food was awful.

I told them I ate sixty percent of my breakfast, but I didn't touch my food. None of the adults would answer any of my questions. I learned how to act by watching the other girls. Dub liked to read, and she got into this argument with some floor nurses about being allowed to read a hardcover book. She agreed to only read it in the day room. We aren't allowed to have hardcover books. I told her she should cut the covers off to make it a soft-cover book. She didn't want to do that though.

China

China wouldn't tell me her story of how she ended up here. She loved talking. She came the same night I did. We jumped on each other's beds, even though we weren't allowed to. We played a ton of Spoons, Uno, and Monopoly. China started to drift away from our group of girls towards the end. At one point, I had a pet snail, which I found in the courtyard. I named him Albert. China crushed him, and I was devastated.

Cat

Cat slept in the bed next to mine. She had been raped in fifth grade, and it was filmed by her classmates. She had also been assaulted by several relatives. She was a freshman. She had cuts running up and down both her arms. She told me she hadn't spent more than five hours at home in the past month because she was constantly in hospitals. She explained that her mom was embarrassed about her scars, so her mom always makes her wear long sleeves in public. She told me that she heard voices, especially in the hospital. I enjoyed giving her life advice, not that she listened. She was good at playing Speed. She brought in a knife and taped it under her arm, so she could cut herself. She would go into the office to ask for tape, but one of the nurses found the knife and held her down and took it. Someone had snitched on her.

They found the knife on her sixth day. I bet she will be here for two weeks, which is the maximum amount of time they can legally hold you for.

Blue

Blue was pretty chill. She was fourteen. On the first day, she told us she was a senior, which I later found out was a lie. I liked her. She was quite a fighter, and she would fight if she ever got mad or upset. She was a marijuana wax dealer and a gang member, and she taught me how to say peace using her gang's sign language. We had a paper-ball fight, which was pretty epic. She had symmetrical razor scratches going up and down her wrists.

Asian Kay

Asian Kay also slept in my room. I let her borrow my slides. She called me cracker. That annoyed me because of the connotation of that word. Asian Kay had a crush on one of the staff members, and when I told him that she had called me cracker, he laughed. I was offended. To pass the time, I also told the guy she liked him, and I asked for his number. He didn't give it to me though. We found out he still lived with his parents, even though he was in his late twenties. I told Asian Kay that she needed someone who could take care of themselves. We played a lot of Speed, and she kept beating me. Asian Kay tried to commit suicide by standing on a train track, but one of her friends found her via Find My Friends and pulled her off the track. Asian Kay did a lot of bed-jumping with China and me, and once, the staff member she had a crush on saw us, but he was pretty chill with it. He pretended he hadn't seen us.

Thorn

There are two facilities here where they keep minors. The other facility is a co-ed one, and the one I am in is all-girls. The other facility is used to keep minors that are involved in crimes and are being held in custody. The girls here call it the "bad place."

Thorn migrated from the bad place with another girl on my second day. Thorn left her "lover," so she was sad about that and wanted to return. We called her Thorn because, on her first day, she was wearing a jacket with a rose on it. She told us that over there, at the "bad place," they didn't get any snacks and didn't have any cards to play. Thorn was in for burglary. I thought Thorn was fairly down to earth. She spoke Spanish, and I spoke some with her. We played a bunch of Spoons.

Jennifer

Jennifer kept calling me gringa, and we would tease all the nurses and therapists by speaking Spanish in front of them. Half of what we said consisted of bad-mouthing the nurses or the therapists. It was a way to pass the time. Jennifer was the oldest girl there. She never got a nickname. I taught her how to play Apples to Apples and Spoons. We also attempted to teach some of the other girls Spanish, so we could use it as a secret code to talk about things that the nurses wouldn't understand.

Other Interesting Stories

All the days kind of meshed together in my mind, which is why I don't have clear divides like my other entries. Throughout the sixty-four hours, in order to fit in, I had to change the way I spoke. I live in an affluent community, and I speak with proper grammar. Most of the girls were from downtown Los Angeles or other parts of the city where the culture is dramatically different. I had to hide my origins. I accomplished this by throwing improper grammar into my speech and altering my accent. I call it my ghetto accent, which I realize is offensive, but I had to appear tough.

Every day, we would have three rotations of floor staff. Each rotation had three members. One of the members would be a nurse, and the other two seemed to be undergrad students who needed to accumulate hours working in a professional setting. I never saw the same people more than once. My favorite floor staff was the second to last staff that I had during my time in the hospital.

The head was this lady dressed in all-white fancy clothes. She was awesome because she let us borrow her nail polish. That staff rotation also let us go into each other's rooms. In the facility, there were three open rooms. Two were rooms with about six beds in each, and the third room was what we called the day room. The day room had a large table, and chairs around its perimeter.

One of the other staff members let us play catch with oranges in the courtyard. We had an abundance of oranges because they always let us have fruit. When the oranges cracked, we threw them over the wall of the compound. That was a nice way to release built-up tension.

We made some paper airplanes and threw them over the wall of the compound into the courtyard. That same awesome staff let us make paper airplanes and throw them at each other.

The morning before I left, a therapist was leading our last group-therapy session. She kept trying to convince us to tell her the story behind why we were each locked up, but none of the girls felt like talking, and those who did would answer her questions with only one word. I got annoyed. I told her to stop asking provoking questions because it would just anger us. I started speaking to Jennifer in Spanish. I told the lady that Jennifer didn't speak any English, so I had to translate everything she was saying, but I was really gossiping about the lady to Jennifer. Right before the lady left, she said, "Gracias," and that cracked me up because her accent was so American.

General Rules
  ◊   We weren't allowed to go in the other rooms or on any bed that wasn't ours
  ◊   Sometimes we were allowed outside in the courtyard
  ◊   The curtain between the bathroom and sleeping quarters always had to stay open
  ◊   No liquids
  ◊   No weapons
  ◊   No plastic
  ◊   No hard-covered books

Los Angeles: Sunday, December 23rd, 2018
I wake up bursting with enthusiasm because I want to get out of the hellhole. I conclude that I am never ever going to forgive my parents for locking me away in this place. I am seething with resentment, which is directed towards them. I feel like a volcano

that is about to erupt. It is time to leave. My mom picks me up, and I am sad to leave my friends. A doctor walks us out, and my mom and I don't say a word to each other, but the second he leaves we start screaming at each other.

My mom tells me that she has spent a ton of time trying to get me out of the hospital. Maybe now she will listen to me. I feel this hatred for my parents that I can't escape from, but I have to put my life back in order.

I am supposed to babysit the girls, but I am not in a healthy mindset. As soon as I return home, I shut myself into my room. My sister keeps coming to check up on me. I missed her, and from what my parents have told me, my sister was distraught after I left. On Friday, she didn't get out of bed to go to school. She also cleaned up the puddle of blood on my bathroom floor the night I ended up in the hospital. While I couldn't care less about my parents, I care about my sister, and I will do what I can to protect her.

Los Angeles: Monday, December 24th, 2018
I ask my sister if she feels like my mom is giving her enough attention and affection, and of course she says no. My mom is so focused on taking care of me

right now that she is practically ignoring my little sister. Ironically, I don't want anything to do with my mom.

I refuse to go to my grandpa's for Christmas Eve dinner. Despite the fact that I am not talking to my mom right now, she feels like she can't leave me alone on Christmas Eve, so she decides to stay home with me. We go to the grocery store, and I buy some junk food, but my mom says, "You need to pay for the crap you buy." I normally don't buy my own food. I have money, so it isn't too bad.

What further irritates me is that my mom refuses to make a decision on the duration of which she is confiscating my car. She claims she wants to talk about it with a family therapist, so we will be doing that the day after Christmas.

When I return home, I lock myself in my room and eat an entire pecan pie. I also play with my rat. I can tell that my mom is scared, and when she's scared, she tightens her control over me that is making me go crazy. My sister returns home at 10:30 at night, and she says she is afraid that I will "disappear again." She convinces me to let her spend the night in my bed. She falls asleep in my arms.

Los Angeles: Tuesday, December 25th, 2018
It's Christmas. I can't stand my parents. I am looking forward to family therapy because I can't live like

this. Family therapy is tomorrow. I guess I kind of enjoy opening gifts alone in my room. My parents are stressed over the whole cutting thing, so they sleep in. My siblings and I decide to make breakfast.

I have decided that because I want my car back, I have to be somewhat reasonable with my parents. I am trying to broker a peace agreement of sorts. My parents can't come up with a decision about the car because according to our stupid-ass contract, I can't drive for like six months. All I did wrong was forget to tell my parents that I drove a friend, and lately, I have had so much on my plate. I just genuinely forgot to tell my parents. I keep receiving mixed messages from my parents. They need to make up their minds. Like, grow up and be parents.

Los Angeles: Wednesday, December 26th, 2018
I stayed up until late last night because I was busy working on school stuff. My parents and I leave my house around 2:15 to go to family therapy, but when we get to the place my dad turns around in his seat to face me and tells me that I am going to a recovery center. My parents blatantly lied to me, and I ask them to take me home, but they want me to go in for two hours.

Like hell I am going to. I storm out of the car and walk four blocks to the library. I turn my phone on airplane mode, so my parents can't track me via Find

My Friends. I spend a few hours reading a book, and then I walk to the beach and then home. It takes me two hours and forty-five minutes to walk home. I am fuming the entire time. I spend the whole time thinking about how upset and frustrated I am.

As I am walking, my dad pulls up because he has been driving around looking for me, and I refuse to get in the car because I don't want him to take me back to the psych ward. My parents have lost my trust. Why would they betray me like that? I am never ever trusting them again.

Los Angeles: Friday, December 28th, 2018

I slept two hours last night because I was fuming with anger. My dad came in to apologize, but that was more of a lecture than anything else. Then I spent three hours talking to my mom, and we established that she will return my car once school starts as long as I spend one hour at the recovery center.

I play Unstable Unicorns, a card game, with my sister.

I receive some good news, though. Sandro Monteblanco calls and tells us that the superior prosecutor decided to press charges and that our case is going to court. Yay, Vicente will be labeled as a rapist for the rest of his life, but this further complicates things. I need to be able to focus on my mental health, and that is difficult when the case is always a part of me.

Los Angeles: Saturday, December 29th, 2018

I go to sleep around two in the morning, and I sleep until 1:30 in the afternoon. My mom wakes me up because she thinks I am dead. Last night, I finished boxing and putting away all of the Christmas decorations, the tree included. I am working on developing clear communication with my mom because I want my car back, and if I don't at least pretend to like her, I won't be allowed to drive.

I agree to spend one hour at the recovery center. I talk to this girl who was raped when she was sixteen. I meet a lot of other survivors; however, there is no way in hell I am going to that place and doing their program that my mom wants me to do. The program is five hours a day for an entire month. I don't have that time with school and homework. Therapy three times a week is enough. When I return home, I am so stressed out that I spend six hours organizing every single drawer in my bedroom.

JANUARY

Los Angeles: Thursday, January 3rd, 2019
Last night, Lola ended up sleeping over. Due to the constant obsessive organizing that I have been doing late at night, it is unrealistic for me to fall asleep before two in the morning. Lola's mom wants her to go to sleep at eleven, so I decide to journal in another room, but then Bryan wants to FaceTime Lola on my phone because Lola doesn't have an iPhone. There is something happening between them. Around midnight, Bryan calls me so he can speak to Lola. I wake her up and let her talk to Bryan in my room.

I leave them for around an hour, but when I come back Lola is crying. I force her to hang up on him. Lola tells me that she had been talking to Bryan, and he left her this sweet voicemail telling her that he liked her. I feel like Lola is unable to decipher her feelings. I'm not convinced she herself even knows what she feels for him. If they end up dating, I don't know what I will do because Lola is one of my closest friends outside school and Bryan is one of my closest friends at school, and he has supported me with the case stuff. I can't be selfish and keep them apart, but I have so much already going on that I don't think I can handle more drama in my life.

Los Angeles: Friday, January 4th, 2019

I wake up in the middle of the night in order to finish my science lab on the pros and cons of dams, which I am way behind on. I finish before I go out to breakfast with a friend. We get crepes! I buy my next journal and a formal dress in case I decide to go to formal this year, which is unlikely because dances are not my thing.

My mom picks me up and drives me to meet with a new therapist because she fired the last one after all the cutting stuff. I like my new therapist. She is older than my last one, and she seems wiser. It takes the whole session to catch her up with everything that has happened in the last six months, and even then I don't get through explaining everything. Every time I talk to someone about the rape, I sound like a broken record. She gives me some good advice on how to handle my feelings for Gabe. She suggests that I write down what I would say to him if I were allowed to speak to him. I haven't done that yet.

Los Angeles: Saturday, January 5th, 2019

Peanut disappoints me today by chewing a hole in my journal.

I go to the Riviera with Camila and Bryan, and I introduce them to Unstable Unicorns. I am proud of myself because they both say they enjoyed the game. We convince Bryan to go to Green Temple, a vegan restaurant that Camila and I love. Then we walk to King Harbor, which is twenty minutes away. We spend an hour in the arcade, and I win two parrot stuffed animals from a claw machine game. I can still be a kid despite how quickly I have had to grow up in the last six months.

After Bryan leaves, Camila and I buy boba and walk back to her house to chill. Her parents are cooking a week's worth of vegetables, and her house has an amazing aroma. Her father is a great cook. I can't stop thinking about all the ways he manages to make vegetables taste good.

Los Angeles: Sunday, January 13th, 2019

It has been six months since the rape. I am upset because I thought I would feel better after six months. I tell the story of how I was raped like a story in a book that I can open and close and put back on the shelf when I am done. All the emotions that I should feel when I think about what happened to me come out in different aspects of my life, rather than during case-related stuff. I feel emotions when I think about the psych ward, Elliott, or Lola and Bryan, but nothing when thinking about the rape.

Today is disappointing because I thought I would feel different—better, maybe. I don't know. Will I feel like this for the rest of my life? I should be able to just get over this, but that is proving to be impossible.

Los Angeles: Tuesday, January 15th, 2019

I started family therapy with this new shrink last week, and I have concluded that he is better than the last family therapist. Last week, I ended up crying and admitting to my father that I still feel hurt by him forcing me to go to Minnesota when I was twelve. I didn't realize that for the last four years I have been harboring feelings of anger against my dad.

When I was in sixth grade, during Thanksgiving break, my family went to Florida. The first night we were in the hotel, my brother and I had a huge fight, and I started hitting him with a sock monkey. My dad told me that if I hit him one more time, he would fly me back to California. I did, and the next morning I was on my way with my dad to Los Angeles; however, the following morning he woke me up and told me we were going to Minnesota. He did this without first asking permission from my mom, and he spent a week taking me to various places that affected him during his childhood: the trailer where he grew up with a single, alcoholic mother, his high school, the grocery store where he got his first job, and the place he worked until he could save up his money to move out of his home and start a life for himself.

Anyway, family therapy just brought back a storm of old memories. I haven't been journaling every day because I have been so busy studying for midterms, which are next week. I am not that stressed out about midterms.

Los Angeles: Saturday, January 19th, 2019

I go out to lunch with my dad and grandpa. I love my grandpa, and he is always there for me, but it's evident that he grew up in a different time period. I enjoy spending time with my grandpa. I wish that I had even more time to hang with him. He has taught me so much, and he tells excellent stories. I will never forget when he told me about his adventures in a nudist colony. His lesson was that you shouldn't judge someone by the materialist things they own.

I have picked up a new hobby: guitar. I want to be able to play guitar and sing along. If I can play every day for a month, I will use my babysitting money to buy myself a sleek, black, acoustic guitar. I find that playing music helps me express and process my emotions.

Los Angeles: Wednesday, January 23rd, 2019

Midterms are over. I am excited to start my semester break.

Everything with my family is always so last minute. I get home from my last midterm, and just as I am parking, my mom calls me. She says that I have a Skype interview with a Peruvian reporter in an hour. I have done this a dozen times before, but it has been a while since I recounted the rape itself. I am surprised at the amount of questions I am asked about the logistics of what happened to me. I thought that I was done with questions like that. It's been over six months, for goodness' sake. My parents have developed a staged lighting system in the living room for these last-minute interviews.

Los Angeles: Sunday, January 27th, 2019

The show about my case airs tonight in Peru, and it is fifteen minutes of amazing work.

In two days, my mom is flying back to Peru to do some follow-up stuff. The news report focuses on talking about the errors of the first prosecutor, and how she had been swayed off what should have been a clear indictment. I once again get to recount the events of the rape and explain how slowly I have been recovering. At the end of the news report, the reporter goes on a rant about how wearing slutty clothing doesn't mean that someone is asking for sex, or in my case, to be raped. Not that I was wearing "slutty clothing" (I was wearing jeans and a sweatshirt), but I appreciate her enthusiasm.

Los Angeles: Wednesday, January 30th, 2019

My mom is in Peru, and I am annoyed because I wanted to go with her. What if she gets murdered? My mom meets the judge, and she receives good vibes from him. My lawyer also thinks the judge is a quality person. The sketchy part of the meeting is when the judge tells my mom that she no longer has to go to the media. Well, we won't have to as long as he does his job. The judge also tells my mom he will be fair, but given the past history with this case, it's hard to trust people when they can be silenced or bought off. At the end of their meeting, the judge gives my mom a hug that surprises my lawyer, but he says it is a good thing.

FEBRUARY

Los Angeles: Friday, February 1st, 2019
I am not allowed to eat anything this morning because I am having my wisdom teeth removed. For the operation, I am being put under. Right after surgery, I can't talk because my tongue and bottom lip are still numb. I take some funny videos of me trying to speak.

I don't go to school, but I spend the afternoon hanging with my neighbor. During the evening, I go to the Riviera to hang out with some Chadwick friends at James' house. None of my girlfriends can make it to the hangout. We have dinner at Good Stuff. My friend group and I eat at Good Stuff a lot because it is a spectacular restaurant chain and we love the atmosphere there.

James has to FaceTime his ex, so the rest of us go to the beach to get out of his hair. Bryan and I go swimming. When I put my jacket back on, it is soaked through with water, so Bryan lets me use his jacket. I think Bryan is flirting with me. I have never had a boy give me his jacket before. It smells like him too. Towards the end of the night, my mouth starts to hurt, and my face begins to swell up and make me look like a chipmunk, but luckily that starts after I leave James' house. Elliott straight-up ignores me the whole night, but it's fine because at least I have Bryan.

Los Angeles: Monday, February 4th, 2019

Other than hanging out with my friends, last week-end was hell. My mouth hurt so much, and I spent the weekend in bed. On Saturday, I texted Gabe happy birthday without my parents' permission, and before I could block him again, he asked me if we were still a couple. Oh, right, I had blocked him before we clarified that we were no longer dating. I thought blocking him would make that apparent. I guess it wasn't to him.

I tell my mom, and she starts crying. I think she is just overwhelmed. She tells me that I have to text him to tell him that I don't have feelings for him and that whatever our relationship is, it needs to end. My mom makes the mistake of talking to my dad about me texting Gabe, which results in a family fight. The only good thing that comes out of family fights is the truth. I learn that my mother talked to my host dad while she was in Peru, and my host dad asked my mom to let me contact Gabe on his birthday. My mother told him no. Of course, my mom wasn't planning on telling me about her conversation, but little did my mom know that I would contact him anyway.

I am tired of my parents withholding information from me. They claim it's for my emotional well-being, but I would rather there be transparency. I have gone through enough. I have the right to know what's going on.

I have therapy and that calms me down a little, but afterwards we have a family dinner. Dinner turns into a family argument, which ends when I storm out of the house to hang with Lola. My house is a war zone!

Los Angeles: Tuesday, February 5th, 2019
Today my parents and I drag my siblings to family therapy. My brother gets upset and storms out of the room within the first five minutes, but he comes back towards the end. My entire family agrees that I am metaphorically the sun of the family and everything revolves around me because of the rape. We also talk about the stupid argument that my parents are having.

I blame myself for the rape. It has had a drastic negative impact on my family. Sometimes I just wish that I never told anyone what happened because I can't stand watching my family suffer on my account.

My sister says that because of the chaos in our household she is always trying to be perfect so that she doesn't take away any time from the case. The good thing that comes out of the family therapy session is that my brother tells us he asked a girl whom we all adore to formal.

Los Angeles: Wednesday, February 6th, 2019
The start of the day is somewhat decent; however, during dinner my mom tells me that despite promising not to tell anyone about the cutting, she went off and told my lawyer and the judge of the case the last time she was in Peru. I'm hurt, and I feel betrayed that she didn't ask for my permission. Probably because she knew the likelihood of me giving it to her was slim. I thought my life was my story to tell. That's not true. Everyone keeps saying that I should control the narrative. I can't. Now I don't trust her. She assures me she didn't tell them about the hospitalization. But how do I know that she didn't? That place still haunts my dreams.

Last week after my parents and I had the argument over texting Gabe on his birthday, I explicitly asked them if they were keeping anything else from me because up until that point, my mom had kept the conversation she'd had with my host dad a secret. My mom assured me that she had told me everything. Well, that was a bald-faced lie. They lied about this in family therapy.

My mom also tells me that shortly after Beto Ortiz's show aired, a girl came into my lawyer's office and lifted up her sleeves. She had scars running up and down both of her arms. She said she had been raped and wanted him to warn my family. Hmm, I would have liked to know about that when my mom found out, not weeks later.

I storm out of the house. Then Bryan FaceTimes me, and we talk for a little. He helps me realize I don't turn to anyone for help, and that I need to close the door on the Gabe stuff. He is right on both accounts.

Los Angeles: Thursday, February 14th, 2019

I believe that even if people are single, they should still celebrate Valentine's Day because you can love someone in a platonic way. There should be more love in the world.

I hang out with Lola because it is her sixteenth birthday until get kicked out of her house because she hasn't finished her homework. She still can't make up her mind about the guys in her life. I wish that was the most pressing concern in my life. She has no idea how lucky she is. I am tired of living this dual life.

I memorized "Blackbird," a fingerpicking song on the guitar. It brings back memories of my time in the psych ward because one of the stupid therapist ladies played it. Anything that reminds me of that place triggers memories of the rape. My best guess is that many of the flashbacks are connected to the hospitalization and the rape because in both of the situations I lacked control. I wish that I had better communication with my parents in December, which might have prevented the events that transpired. If anyone has negative thoughts or is using unhealthy coping mechanisms like I used cutting, they should tell a trusted adult. Had I been able to better communicate my feelings, I wouldn't have gone through the hell that I went through.

Los Angeles: Saturday, February 16th, 2019

I wake up in a bad mood. I obsessively clean my room, and I spend some of the time with my mom. I also think that I am starting to like Bryan because I get jealous when he hugs Camila, which isn't even a romantic thing.

I am a little closed off from my mom, given that she hasn't earned back my trust. I tell her how I think therapy is starting to feel like a waste of time.

I attempt to open up to my mom and tell her that even though it's been two months, I still have haunting dreams and flashbacks of my time in the psych ward. She goes on this rant about how she didn't know what to do and how it was my fault that I ended up there. All I want her to do is listen and let me talk because I'm not talking to any of my friends about the hospital, and I just need someone to listen while I vent. I tell her to stop talking, but she keeps on talking. She calls me a bitch and tells me to get out of the car and walk home. Granted, it is only a ten-minute walk home, so I shouldn't complain.

I have to babysit as soon as I return home. I don't talk to my mom again. This is why I can't talk to her, or anyone for that matter because they just won't understand. I feel like I have no one to talk to right now.

Guess who gets to go back to Peru? This time my whole family is going. Sandro Monteblanco tells us that we are invited by a Peruvian congressman to speak to the Congress of Peru about sexual assault. My parents decide that we are going to Belize on the way down to Peru. I am nervous about returning to Peru. I hate dragging my siblings into the middle of this.

Los Angeles: Sunday, February 17th, 2019
This morning I start to stress out and clean my room again. Bryan is coming over, but I also invited Lola.

They show up around twelve, and I have to leave two hours later because of a friend's sweet sixteen celebration. Lola spends the time flirting with Bryan, and for some reason it upsets me. Correction, it hurts me because I like him, but of course I can never tell either of them that or act on my feelings considering I dated his cousin, Elliott, who now won't even talk to me.

I'd hoped we could all hang out as a group of friends without any awkward romance, but no. I feel like I have lost both of their friendships because they would rather spend time together than hang in a group. Lola kicks me out of my own room to spend some alone time with Bryan. I want to be happy for both of them, but I'm struggling with that. Bryan and Lola stay at my house for a couple of hours after I leave. They are so lucky that neither of my parents are home.

While I am at the celebration, Lola texts me because she can't figure out her feelings. I feel like she is taking Bryan for granted. He is such an amazing guy, and part of me thinks that my dumb self from a year ago chose the wrong cousin. To be fair, I barely knew Bryan back then.

Los Angeles: Wednesday, February 20th, 2019
I should be happy because I don't have school today, but I can't stop thinking about yesterday. I think I

like Bryan, but for obvious reasons I can't do anything about it. Lola texts me, and we walk to the local coffee shop. Lola keeps saying how Bryan reminds her too much of her father, so she can't be with him. I listen to her rant for an hour. She doesn't understand how much he means to me even though I know nothing romantic can happen between us. I feel like she is toying with his emotions, and both of them are my closest friends. I don't know what to do.

She keeps rubbing this secret she has with him in my face, and she won't tell me what it is. It is starting to really annoy me. My guess is she did something sexual with Bryan but won't outwardly tell me what it is. Not that I care. I guess it doesn't matter. It's one thing to keep a secret, but it's another to tell someone you have a secret and then emphasize their not knowing what it is, just to make yourself feel better.

When I return home, I am just frustrated. I write a song to express myself. It's just one more thing I can't show anyone. Of course, the song is about my feelings for Bryan.

I go out to have coffee with my mom. I vent a little about Bryan and Lola. My vent ends with both of us crying, but I need to express to someone the loss of my two closest friends. Now, I need people more than ever, but I feel like everyone is consumed by their own lives, so they have no time to be there for me.

Los Angeles: Thursday, February 21st, 2019

I am feeling a little better today. I don't know what to say to Bryan because I don't want to talk to him about Lola. I want to distance myself from his and Lola's relationship. I can't keep torturing myself by being the middle person. Every time I see them, I get a little jealous. It does help that Lola goes to a different school. Last night, I clarified to myself that it's not that I have a crush on Bryan. It's that if he and Lola are together, I lose two of my best friends. I am trying not to be selfish, so I won't say anything to either of them. I feel like I have lost their attention, which is what I need the most right now.

While I am trying to distance myself from the two of them, Bryan tells me that he needs to talk to me because he feels like Lola is flirting with someone else. Why do I get the impression he is using me? When he has her, he relies on her, and when she is unavailable, he comes to me. I feel like Lola flirts with every guy she encounters. There isn't anything wrong with that, but Bryan deserves better than Lola, and he sure as hell deserves someone better than me.

Around 7:30 at night, Lola calls me and tells me that Bryan has friend-zoned her. I'm proud of him for that because she is a little too crazy for him. They are just so different. Of course, my friends' happiness is the most important thing to me. I feel like there is more to this story. I love my platonic relationships with Bryan and Lola, but having relationships with both of them, is so draining.

Los Angeles: Friday, February 22nd, 2019

Bryan and I have an argument during lunch about holding grudges. Bryan proceeds to bring up the fact that Elliott is still mad at me despite the fact that it has been five months. Yeah, like I don't already know that he is still mad at me, and the best part is I don't know why he's mad at me. He wouldn't tell me why he was upset in October, and now it's February and he still hasn't talked to me about it. I have been a little too preoccupied dealing with the case stuff to try to win back Elliott's friendship.

I don't believe in holding grudges because I think they are unproductive and immature. For some reason, Bryan bringing up the Elliott stuff pushes me to the point where I send him a text explaining my views on the topic. The anger sits with me for the entire day, just residing in my gut.

My mom and I go for coffee, and she helps me craft a script for what I should say to Elliott in the hopes of figuring out why he is mad at me. He has been mad at me since October. It's about time that I address this. I just wish he told me why he is mad. I thought friends communicate with each other. I guess we haven't been friends for a while.

Los Angeles: Saturday, February 23rd, 2019
I didn't sleep well last night because I was worrying about how to apologize to Elliott. I tell my dad about my plan. He exclaims that what my mom advised me to say is stupid. My dad and Elliott share some similar qualities. When they get mad at someone, they ignore them and don't communicate their feelings for a long period of time. Granted, my dad has gotten better at communicating in a timely manner because of all the family therapy my mom and I have dragged him to. My relationship with my father is more important than whatever I have with Elliott. Also, like my dad, Elliott is very stubborn and set in his own ways. I don't believe in grudges. If you care about someone, you have to be able to forgive and move forward.

Elliott hasn't talked to me in five months, and my dad understands how people can hold grudges. My dad's advice is to make the conversation less about me and more about Elliott. He says I am focusing too much on me and not enough on Elliott's feelings. My dad helps me realize that with guys, no matter how many times you apologize, once they go off a cliff, only they can make the decision to climb up again.

I call Elliott. He was sleeping, but he tells me that if I have something important to say I should talk to him in person. The brief conversation just makes me more anxious. Why do I still care about this?

I talk to Bryan for a while, and he feels like Lola is ignoring him. We are both flowing through upset mindsets. With Bryan's permission, I walk to Lola's house and tell her that Bryan feels that she is ignoring him, and now they are back to their blissful heaven. At least two of us are happy!

Los Angeles: Sunday, February 24th, 2019
I didn't do any homework, and now I have to suffer. I finish all my homework in around four hours.

Then I babysit for the girls. They are little jubilant bundles of energy. I don't understand why little kids like me so much. It doesn't make any sense. The girls and I make up this new game based on the premise of the book series *Fablehaven* and create our own twists. One twist is that there is this willow tree that opens a door into a magical realm with good and evil creatures, and by opening the portal to the magical realm, evil is released into the human world.

After babysitting, I have therapy. I can't get Elliott out of my mind. I spend the whole therapy session talking about him. Because I am in Manhattan Beach anyway, I want to drive to Elliott's house to talk to him in person, so I call Bryan to ask if he knows what his cousin is up to. Bryan tells me that Elliott is at football practice. I think the universe is telling me what a bad idea apologizing is.

MARCH

Los Angeles: Friday, March 1st, 2019

Even though today is a Friday, I am able to sleep in because I don't have school. I tell myself that I am going to be productive, but that doesn't happen. I watch about three hours of Netflix.

I go over to Elliott's house with the hopes that I can work up the guts to apologize to him for what I did. I still don't know what that is because he hasn't told me. Camila bails on the hangout. She has a tendency to bail on friend group hangouts. I apologize to Elliott, but it feels awkward because the rest of my friends ditch us, and it feels like a setup. I have no idea why I am trying so hard to fix what is broken. Should I keep trying or just give up?

I wish I could lock away my emotions and become a human robot because then I wouldn't care. It's frustrating that despite everything that has happened, I still care about Elliott. Three months ago, I would have been fine with continuing to ignore him, but something has changed inside me. Maybe it's because I have gone cold turkey on my antidepressant medication and sleeping pills. I am regaining the full spectrum of emotions, and it sucks.

Los Angeles: Sunday, March 2nd, 2019

My friend group planned on meeting at a Coffee Bean, but everyone bailed except one of my friends who isn't really a part of my friend group. I decide to have coffee with her one-on-one. After drinking some coffee, we spontaneously decide to go buy her a pet rat, but Petco doesn't have any left, and I have to leave to meet all the friends who bailed on Coffee Bean at my house. I think the day that I brought my rat to school inspired her to buy one of her own. That was a good day. I was popular for once.

My guy friends and I play spike ball until Camila and Lola come over. We hang out, and somehow Bryan and I end up jumping into the freezing pool. Bryan is mad at me because I keep teasing him about Lola, and I apologize. I am surprised that Elliott came over because lately he has been ditching our hangouts. I thought he didn't want anything to do with me. Bryan uses my blanket as a towel which annoys me, and Elliott accidently drops chips all over my room. I should make a no-food policy in my room.

Los Angeles: Friday, March 15th, 2019

I think I like Bryan. He claims he is over Lola. Regardless, nothing romantic can happen between us because that would break the girl code because of Lola and the cousin code because of Elliott. Bryan spends an hour convincing me he is over Lola, but I don't buy it. I dare him to kiss one of the random girls who is hanging out with us at that moment. Then I realize how much it would hurt me if they were to kiss right in front of me. Thankfully, he refuses my dare. Had both he and the girl accepted my dare, I would have been quite uncomfortable.

I babysit for Rafe. His mom knows about the Peru stuff because every time I babysit him, I always spend some time talking to her when she returns home. Rafe's mom is also a survivor of sexual assault. She can help me in many ways others can't. When I talk to her, I feel like she understands what I am going through. Now, she has become a mentor to me. I hope that when I'm older I will be able to be as strong as she is. She survived, so I know that I can as well. She also gives me advice, and she tells me that she is worried that if I don't find an outlet, I won't be able to recover. I agree, but I feel like people close to me are tired of hearing me talk about the case. She was able to move on and start a new life in California after her rape. I, on the other hand, have to finish high school. She has helped me realize that with the case hanging over my head, I will be unable to move on with my life. I can't stop now. We won't have a verdict for months. I don't know how to help myself. My "good days" are manageable, but my "bad days" are awful.

Los Angeles: Saturday, March 16th, 2019

I can't get over liking Bryan. This causes so many problems. There is no way I will do anything. I am his cousin's ex, and he and my best out-of-school friend have a thing. I literally check my phone every five seconds hoping to receive a text from him. To make matters worse, his cousin still won't talk to me, and I have decided I will wait no longer. I have to burn that bridge for my own sake.

Bryan and I FaceTime for three hours, and I am keeping the hospitalization a secret from him, but I feel guilty because I keep hinting at it because I want to talk to someone about it, which is stupid. I am aching to talk to someone about it, but this is one secret that I have to keep. What am I going to do with my feelings? I can't tell him. I have dropped too many hints already, such as telling him that I was jealous when he hugged Camila. I'm sure he is picking up on it, and he is just such an amazing person. He deserves someone better than me. I also hate how much pain Lola drags him through.

Los Angeles: Monday, March 18th, 2019

One more week until Spring Break. We are going to fly to Belize on our way down to Peru. James and I are becoming closer friends. Bryan, James, and I go out to dinner together. Of course, my feelings for Bryan won't go away, and it's getting more difficult to hide them. I feel like I will slip up soon. God, if you exist, although you probably don't, please help me destroy my feelings for him. My life is difficult enough as it is. My grades are on a downward spiral, and normally I wouldn't care; however, I don't have a single A right now. There is still time left in the year to pull them back up.

I have therapy, and I feel like I am able to truly open up. I talk to my therapist about all the pieces that landed me in the psych ward. She seems to understand better than anyone else. I think she is able to realize that I went to the psych ward furious with my parents, and I came out equally if not more infuriated with my parents. In hindsight, what good did it do? It just spurred new nightmares and flashbacks of my rape. If I wanted to kill myself, I easily could have done so in the psych ward. One of the girls in my room had a knife taped under her arm.

Los Angeles: Tuesday, March 19th, 2019

I guess I am writing because I have to vent, and it's not like I can vent to my friends for various reasons. My issue is that I like Bryan, which is complicated by the fact that he is my closest friend. I am so happy whenever he texts or calls me because it makes me feel like at least someone cares about me.

Bryan leaves school early today. I hang out with James. We go walking in the canyon. I tell him about what happened to me in Peru. I think that my explanation of what happened helps him understand me better. He is too nice of a person to dig deep into another person's life, so while he heard Bryan and I talk about the court case in the past, he never questioned what we were discussing. Why can't I have feelings for someone like James, where liking him wouldn't break any code? Never mind he is also one of Elliott's friends, but at least he isn't Elliott's cousin.

Bryan FaceTimes me and we talk about Lola like normal. Whenever I talk about the two of them together, it makes me jealous, but I think I do a pretty decent job of hiding my true feelings. I wonder how much longer I will be able to bottle up my feelings.

Los Angeles: Thursday, March 21st, 2019
I don't go to school because I only have projects due, and I am more productive working at home.

Yesterday, I talked to Bryan for three hours. I have to stop hinting at my feelings. I went to school around two to pick up my sister, but Bryan and I decided to hike in the canyon. Elliott and I used to have a secret spot where we would hang out under the football field. I took Bryan there because the view of the city is magnificent. After visiting the spot, Bryan refused to walk up the main road with me. He wanted to time it, so we walked up individually because he didn't want other people to think we were a couple. Why does he care what other people think? They can mind their own business, and all our friends know that the two of us are only friends anyway. His comment insulted me, but I remembered that his cousin felt the same way when we first started going to that spot. They are two peas in a pod.

Bryan asks me who I have a crush on, and I blurt out the first name on my tongue, which happens to be Elliott. I have been thinking about Elliott lately because I am so focused on my quest of apologizing to him. I instantly regret saying that, but it's better than Bryan finding out that I like him.

Los Angeles: Friday, March 22nd, 2019

I walk to Lola's house, and one of her friends is texting her about Bryan. Lola's friend apparently likes Bryan. Let me clarify a few things. Lola has decided that she has feelings for Bryan again, despite already friend-zoning him and already having him friend-zone her. Lola's friend, whom I have never met, recently met Bryan. Lola's friend has no idea that Lola also has feelings for Bryan, and Lola isn't planning on telling her. Even though Bryan claims he's over Lola, I am not convinced that's true. I convince Bryan to text Lola's friend that he wants to be friends with her and nothing more. I spend two hours working on this, while Lola spends the two hours talking about how much she likes Bryan. It's ironic that the two of them have both friend-zoned each other. What should I do? I have to take myself out of the middle of all this drama as soon as possible.

It's a good thing I'm leaving for Belize later tonight. I am nervous because after Belize my family is going to Peru, and my parents and I get to speak to the Congress of Peru. I debate starting to work on my speech for Congress, but I realize that I have some time.

Belize: Saturday, March 23rd, 2019

Once we arrive in Belize, we have five hours to kill before the boat we are chartering is ready. I spend that time sleeping on the couch in the waiting area of the boating office. My dad loves sailing. We charter sail boats, he captains them, and my mom is always the first mate. After my nap, my family plays a round of mini-golf, parents versus kids. After nine holes, the game ends in a tie, which upsets my sister because she wanted a win.

There is Wi-Fi in the boating office, so I call Bryan. I know that Bryan and Lola both talk about me with each other. I can't trust either of them with anything. Clearly, I have to stay out of Bryan and Lola's business, but that's nearly impossible when they both talk to me about one-another. As much as I know I shouldn't let myself be in-between them, I want to be in both of their lives, but being in both of their lives right now causes me tremendous pain. I feel like they are both using me to gain information about the other.

Belize: Monday, March 25th, 2019

As a family, we decide that anytime someone mentions anything about the upcoming Peru trip, I can slap them. Peru is so close, yet I want to bury it so deep that it never sees the sun again.

I wake up at seven because we are going on a dive. Despite having a somewhat hectic dive master, we have a spectacular dive. We are followed around by two nurse sharks. They are like sea puppies who love to be scratched right behind their gills. I see two moray eels, a hawksbill turtle, four eagle rays, three lobsters, and about seven lionfish.

After the dive, we sail to South Water Caye. At South Water Caye, we attempt to find a good snorkeling spot, but that doesn't happen. There is no cell service.

I still can't stop thinking about Bryan, but I have made the executive decision that when I talk to him, I won't mention Lola. I am done putting myself in the middle. I keep saying that, but I feel like I keep bouncing right back in-between them.

Belize: Saturday, March 29th, 2019

It's my last full day, and I slept in, but my siblings went diving. They go spearfishing for lionfish. They come back with this fantastic story. Another person on the dive with them tried to spear a lionfish and missed, which I find incredulous because lionfish are super slow. The lionfish felt threatened and attacked the dive master, who was stung by two barbs. Because of the incident, their second dive was canceled.

We sail to Pelican Caye. There are no restaurants or people, so we cook the lionfish my siblings have speared and eat it on the boat.

My brother and I take a ride on the dinghy, a little nine-horsepower inflatable boat. I fall overboard while going over a wave. I am quite upset, and I blame my brother's lack of dinghy motoring skills. My brother also throws a book at my head. I start crying, not because of the pain, but because I need to cry. I stay in my room for the rest of the night and just let out my emotions.

I contemplate starting my speech for Congress, but I decide not to. I have to been in the right mindset to outline a speech. What am I doing with my life?

Belize: Sunday, March 31st, 2019

We sail for about three hours to get back to the dock. I call Camila, and she tells me that she has kissed a boy. What an exciting tale. While I am at the airport, Bryan calls me. I am glad he called me and not the other way around. We talk for twenty minutes before the flight, but later we talk for two hours while I wait in the airport in Belize City. It turns out Bryan has been hanging out with Lola. Good for him; however, I know Lola hasn't been able to make up her mind about Bryan. Bryan thinks there's a chance of them dating, but he doesn't know Lola like I do. I love Lola, but I admire Bryan. Again, part of me thinks he is too good for her; however, he deserves a shot at happiness with her if he thinks that's possible. I won't try to convince him otherwise, although I can see their inevitable doom.

My brother and I have a deep conversation in which he tells me that I am manipulating Bryan by not telling him about my feelings for him. In a way, I think my brother has a point. I'm a hypocrite because I admire people who are open, honest, and direct. In many ways, I'm not.

APRIL

Peru: Monday, April 1st, 2019

Yay, it's sexual assault awareness month, and I get to spend the first part of it fighting against sexual assault! Life is cruelly ironic sometimes.

While lying in bed from five to six this morning, I contemplate why I keep such an important part of myself hidden from Bryan. For a while, I debate the question of whether or not I have a crush on him. I reach the conclusion that I simply admire him because he is such a wonderful, pure person.

The last person I truly let see me for me was Gabe, but since then I have closed myself off from everyone else. In losing Gabe, I lost the only person I truly trusted: my ultimate outlet. After that loss, disaster struck, and I haven't let myself get close to anyone, either because I feel like people are too busy with their own lives, or because I fear letting them in and then losing them like I did with Gabe. I realize why I am jealous of Bryan and Lola's relationship.

I am envious of the honesty and directness that they have with each other because I know there is part of me that wants to find that. It feels like everyone I trust in some way always betrays me. Once upon a time I had that honesty with Elliott, but after the rape and the subsequent events, I changed, and I lost myself. Only now am I starting to recover bits and pieces of the old me, and I am working on developing the new me. I could never love Bryan in a romantic way. No, that's a lie. I could see myself loving him, but that would be wrong. If I can find it in my heart to open up to him, I will, but only as a trusted friend and outlet. God knows I need one right now.

If I were to rely on Bryan as I did on Gabe and something were to happen to ruin our friendship, I would be devastated. The pain would be all-consuming. I can't have another hospitalization situation. I also realize that during the Gabe stuff, I started to push away my parents. I feel like I could explain why I needed Gabe an infinite amount of times to them, and they still won't understand why and how he played such a significant role in my life. They just saw him as a threat to the case. He cared for me so much, in a way that's very similar to how Bryan cares for Lola, but Lola's idea of a "perfect boyfriend" blinds her from seeing that. She is lucky, and she doesn't know it. I feel like I haven't been honest with myself for a while.

After breakfast, I sit down at the desk in my hotel, and I begin writing my speech for Congress. As I write the speech, I am overcome by waves of emotions. Emotions that I haven't felt about the rape in months. I am used to feeling numb, but as I create my outline, I feel anger and sadness but also strength. I am thankful that these emotions are coming back to me. Five hours later, I look down at my outlined speech, and I feel content and satisfied. When I give speeches, I don't write them out word for word. I like writing down the general ideas. I feel ready. I got this. It's time to help change a country.

Sandro Monteblanco comes to the hotel, and we spend a few hours debriefing the schedule and upcoming plans. I also run through the speech that I created, and he gives me a few more points to add.

First Point
◊ Express gratitude to Alberto De Belaunde, the advisory staff, and the Investigative Commission of Sexual Abuse of Minors in Organizations
◊ Introduce my name and age

◊ "I respect the laws of Peru, but I just want to share how things are done in the United States..."

Second Point

◊ Compare and contrast how Peru and the United States deal with the concept of "re-victimization"

◊ "In the United States, victims are encouraged to be present at their hearing while I was asked not to be present during mine."

◊ "I wanted to meet with everyone involved in the case, but I have come to realize that isn't viable because of the laws supposedly protecting minors, which are inhibiting."

Third Point

◊ I was sad, scared, and embarrassed when I told my family

◊ I have love, support and encouragement, which have helped me move forward

◊ I will not be a silent victim, which is why I decided to tell friends and authorities that Markham College is harboring my rapist

Fourth Point (Create the timeline)

◊ Began the crusade by filling out police report

◊ Meeting with Forensic Psychologists

◊ Testimony with Peruvian Public Ministry

◊ Meetings with the United States Embassy

◊ Interviews with members of the press

Fifth Point

◊ "The toughest aspect of the process is being made to feel like a liar and an aggressor by the Fourteenth Family Public Ministry of Lima under the prosecutor who dismissed the charges because the toxicology results were negative."

◊ This sends a message to silent victims, still living in the shadows, that their voices are invalid

◊ Potential corruption or pressure placed on the prosecutor?

Sixth Point

◊ Address everyone formally

◊ "In Peru, there has been an increase of women being beaten, raped, and murdered, which is why commissions such as De Belaunde's will be vital for implementing important changes—changes that will educate the young and changes that will punish aggressors accordingly."

◊ Changes that will enable and help more girls stand up and speak out

Conclusion

In closing, Peru is a spectacular country. It has an impressive culture, a rich history, and food to die for. Peru needs to be respected and known for those reasons around the world, not for the femicides and violence against women that take place here. I am not asking you to help me find justice: I am asking you to find justice for the silent victims, those with less fortunate circumstances than mine. Thank you for allowing me to have a voice. Thank you to the Peruvian Police, the Doctor of Legal Medicine, Forensic Psychologists, and Beto Ortiz. Thank you to the United States Embassy, and Dr. Rita Figueroa Vásquez, the superior prosecutor who deemed my case fit for trial, for believing in me.

Peru: Tuesday, April 2nd, 2019

I wake up at five because I can't sleep. Sandro Monteblanco, a news reporter, and my family meet in the hotel where we spend time conducting interviews in our room and the conference room. Then we drive to the giant cross on top of the hill that borders the Lima Peninsula to do more filming. My brother and sister do great on camera, and I do a lot of "modeling" for the camera. The film crew asks me to stand and pose. Then we move locations, and I stand and pose again. It's repetitive. I could never be a model. It's just too boring. Our news reporter is super pro-women's rights, but Sandro Monteblanco keeps reminding me, "She is a journalist and not our friend."

After a solid seven hours of interviewing, we drive back to the hotel. I call Bryan, and I tell him about my experiences in the psych ward. He's the first friend of mine I tell. He takes everything well. He also talks about him and Lola. He tells me that the last time they were at my house together, when I left them alone, they made out. It sure took him a while to tell me that especially considering that I heard about it from Lola a while ago.

The Congressional hearing has been moved to Friday. I'm not sure what we are going to do tomorrow.

Peru: Wednesday, April 3rd, 2019

I don't want to drag my lazy butt out of bed this morning. I barely slept last night because I was anxious and nervous. We meet our news reporter at a waterpark and take some footage in a scenic garden.

The gardens are still closed to the public, but we are allowed to enter. We focus on the letter written by the head of my high school explaining what an exemplary student I am.

Then we go to the TV studio and do some filming with a black screen. My siblings stay at the hotel. After filming at the studio, we take a lunch break. Afterwards, we do more filming at the hotel.

In the late afternoon, when we finish, my dad, brother, and I go shopping. I buy an outfit for the meeting with the judge tomorrow.

I call Lola and Camila. Lola is officially dating Bryan. I see their inevitable doom. There is no way it will end up working out. I want to talk to Bryan about it, but I have a meeting with Sandro Monteblanco to prepare for my meeting with the judge tomorrow.

The rapist's lawyer contacted our news reporter, and they want to go on air. Vicente is now eighteen, so he can no longer hide behind closed doors. Sandro Monteblanco thinks Vicente's wealth comes from old money, and that Vicente's parents inherited it. One of the past Peruvian ministers has the same last name as Vicente, so there is a chance that Vicente's family could be related to some influential people. When Sandro Monteblanco did some digging on the rapist's family, he found very little information. Rumor has it that some of the money financing the rapist's defense team is coming from gold mines in a remote region of Peru. The gold mines are owned by the family that hosted the party. They are allegedly helping the rapist's family pay for lawyer fees because they don't want to be sued by my family.

Peru: Thursday, April 4th, 2019

I have to wake up at six to visit the judge. When we arrive at the courthouse, we have to wait two hours. Sandro Monteblanco is told that I can't speak to the judge because it would be too "re-victimizing." At this point, I am as numb as a goldfish.

Sandro Monteblanco and my parents meet with the judge. Ten minutes later Sandro Monteblanco comes running out of the judge's chambers and reports that the judge wants to speak to me. I have gum in my mouth. Sandro is such a saint. There are no trash cans nearby, and he knows that I will have to shake the judge's hand, so he holds my disgusting, chewed-up gum in his hand for me.

The meeting with the judge goes pretty well. The judge remembers that I spend a good amount of my free time babysitting, and he explains that when victims work with little kids, they regain part of their innocence. At one point, he even laughs. At the end of the meeting, the judge gives us all hugs. He seems like he is a haunted man who has seen many horrible and traumatic cases in his life. He also seems sad and weighed down. I'm never going to be a judge.

When we get back to the hotel, I discover that my mom has been lying to me since February. I am looking for photos on my dad's WhatsApp to send to myself. I find a WhatsApp message on the group chat with Sandro Monteblanco, my dad and my mom. In the WhatsApp message, my mom asks Sandro not to tell me that she told him about the hospitalization.

When my mom returns from lunch, I ask her once again if she has told anyone about the hospitalization, and she says no right to my face. Once again, she lies to me. I am so tired, and I have taken melatonin. All I want to do is sleep. My mom can tell I am upset with her. She accuses me of acting like Elliott because I'm not talking to her, and that further infuriates me. Right before I fall asleep, I send her a screenshot of her text to Sandro Monteblanco.

I am never trusting her again. This is the last straw. I keep forgiving her for her lies, and she keeps telling me she is going to stop, but that doesn't appear to be true.

I sleep for five hours, and then, around eight at night, when I am in bed with a face mask on, my brother and sister are fighting in the bathroom because my brother spit toothpaste on my sister. Then my brother won't turn out the lights. We ask him to change and finish getting ready in the bathroom, considering that we have to wake up early tomorrow for Congress, but he is being insensitive and refuses. I tell my dad. My dad manages to lock himself out of his room because my mom is sleeping. My dad blames me for my siblings' fight, and he goes on and on about how selfish I am.

My dad says I am being a bitch and that he doesn't want to go to my hearing with Congress tomorrow, which is the main reason we are in Peru in the first place. I wasn't even the sibling fighting. I start to silently cry. I go into the bathroom and cut myself with a razor on my hip so no one would see. It's not like I can go for a run as a coping mechanism, and cutting is by far the quickest-reacting coping mechanism I know. I know it's bad, but it helps bring down my emotions, and I know that I have to calm down quickly in order to sleep. Maybe I don't have my dad's unconditional support, and I sure as hell don't trust my mom, but at least I have my siblings.

Peru: Friday, April 5th, 2019

I wake up jittery and anxious because I am presenting my speech to the Congress of Peru. I take ten deep breaths and allow my mind to go blank so that my fear doesn't hijack my brain. I tell myself that I can do it. I am prepared. I have practiced my speech multiple times a day since I crafted it.

I am upset because of the events that transpired last night. My dad argues with my mom about coming today. Whatever she says to him, convinces him to come. Even though what my dad said about me last night upsets me, I am relieved that he decides to come. I still love him, and it means the world to me that he is here supporting me. I have to compartmentalize how I feel about my dad's words in order to perform at my best today. Because to some extent, the future of Peru is riding on this speech.

We arrive at the House of Congress early, and Sandro Monteblanco has me run through my speech. When I read it aloud, everyone in the car starts crying except for my dad.

The head of the Congress Commission who invited us to speak is Alberto De Belaunde. My mom speaks first. It is nerve-wracking because we are all seated around a conference table. Alberto De Belaunde is at the head, and near the other end are two different film crews. My whole family is sitting together on chairs around the perimeter of the room. My mom grabs my hand and gives it a squeeze of encouragement. Our reporter's cameraman is focusing on our case, but our reporter can't be here because she is off interviewing my rapist's current lawyer.

I stand up and take two deep breaths. I begin my speech. The words flow right out of me. I have been preparing for this moment. I am holding my outline in my hand, but I barely glance down at it. I know what I have to say. As I speak, my emotions creep their way into my words. It feels surreal. I have given speeches in the past, but this one feels unique. I give this speech with the purpose of making the justice system in Peru better for sexual assault survivors. At the end of the speech, I feel like I am in a daze. My family and lawyer congratulate me. Everyone tells me that I did a great job.

Shortly afterwards, a psychologist from the congressional commission who was wearing all black, comes up to me and says, "Mackenzie, your story was my voice today. I too am a victim of sexual assault." I am speechless. I have no idea what to say, and I don't want to be inconsiderate because she has been with us all day. I am just in shock.

The judge wants to redo the witness testimonies during Easter week. So, none of the witnesses will be able to go out of town. My mom has to be present on April 17th and 24th for those hearings in order to testify.

I meet with an agent from the United States Embassy, and we discuss what steps I will take moving forward. We discuss issues relating to Markham College and Round Square. I am pleased to hear that the United States Embassy has taken Markham College off their approved-schools list for children of United States diplomats. The United States Embassy has helped my family so much. I am tremendously thankful for the United States Embassy agents who have helped my family and me fight for justice. We wouldn't be where we are now without all of their help.

Los Angeles: Sunday, April 7th, 2019

I spend a while reflecting on the speech that I gave to the Peruvian Congress. I feel really good about it. I hope that it persuades the Congress to implement changes in Peru's criminal justice system that benefit sexual assault survivors. I am thankful that my whole family spent a week in Peru supporting me. I know I fought a bit with my parents, but it was a stressful time for everyone. I know that it is in times like these that we actually grow stronger individually and as a family.

In trying to remedy all the lies my mom has told me, she adds me to the WhatsApp chat with Sandro Monteblanco and my dad. Hopefully, this will help keep me informed on the case and prevent her from lying to me about case-related stuff in the future. I forgive my mom for lying to me about the hospitalization stuff because I realize that she was only trying to protect me.

The news airs, and I am annoyed because our reporter went back on her promise that she wouldn't show the WhatsApp messages that Desiree sent Vicente's mother's friend back in August. I understand Sandro Monteblanco's quote: "Journalists aren't our friends."

Vicente goes on air and says in Spanish, "Mackenzie, please tell the truth, not just for me but for my family and my future." I am telling the truth! None of us are feeling good about the story that was aired, but at least Vicente's lawyer looked like an idiot.

Despite the twelve hours of filming, I don't feel like the material was used to make a stellar report.

School starts tomorrow, and I am nervous, but I am also excited to see my friends.

Los Angeles: Monday, April 8th, 2019

After school, I am so tired that I don't want to do anything. My brother has a haircut that I have to drive him to, and then I have therapy, which my mom also comes to because I want my therapist to ease her mind about the cutting. I guess it goes okay, but I find out that my mom has been talking to our family therapist about the cutting too, and for some reason I can't explain I get bad vibes from the family therapist.

My therapist thinks I should learn to rely on other people more, but I don't because I can't trust anyone in my life, especially my mother.

When I return home, I look myself up online and find that four different newspapers have published articles about my case. Some anonymous person from Peru directly messages me through Instagram asking me to stop my fight against my rapist because he is a friend of Vicente's younger brother. Whoever has written the message has decent English, although, it could have easily been Google-translated.

It is direct but polite, which makes me more upset. I hadn't realized the rapist has a younger brother. Am I doing the right thing by continuing this battle?

My lawyer saw my host dad in a coffee shop. My host dad walked up to my lawyer and said hello and told him that he was meeting a client, but then he suspiciously walked out of the shop. My lawyer thinks he was meeting with someone on the rapist's defense council.

Los Angeles: Thursday, April 11th, 2019

At school, I have my advisory meeting where I spend the time dodging questions per usual.

Therapy is more interesting though. It starts with my dad and I yelling at each other, but the family therapist exclaims that we argue like lawyers and we should be talking about our feelings rather than justifying our actions and not listening to one another. We should be using the model "I feel blank when blank because blank." It takes a while to adapt everything I want to say to my dad using the therapist's phrasing. I feel awful because I am talking about how I felt when my dad called me a selfish bitch back in Peru. I hope my dad and I can work on our relationship.

My mom says something that angers my dad, and he declares he will never go back to the family therapist. He uses that line to punish my mom because he knows she thinks family therapy is important.

I feel like we were making some progress, but if my dad bails on therapy, we are just going to go backwards. Next week we won't have therapy because my mom will be testifying in Peru, and I will be stuck at home.

Los Angeles: Friday, April 12th, 2019

The school day goes by quicker than I thought it would. I hang out at James' house with some friends, and guess who shows up? Elliott. He still won't talk to me. I am past the point of caring.

Bryan and Lola ditch us to hang out alone upstairs. I am trying to eradicate my feelings for Bryan, but feelings don't just come and go as I want them to. I feel like I am constantly wearing a mask to protect myself, and the way I act in a group setting isn't the real me.

At the end of the night, James walks me to my car, and we talk for a while. Well, he talks. I mostly listen, but the whole time my mind is lost in memories of my hospitalization. I struggle to keep my emotions in check. He explains to me that he feels like an outsider with his friends. James is quieter than the other boys. I can see that as well. I can relate to how he feels, but I don't want to talk about me because it is obvious he needs someone to just listen to him. I am happy to be that person for him.

Los Angeles: Monday, April 15th, 2019

I guess it is a good day, right up until therapy. The conversation goes deep quickly. I just sit on the couch in the shrink's office with a pretty little smile on my face while inside I am seething with anger. She interrogates me about the cutting and the hospitalization, which at first I am okay with, until she demands that I find another coping mechanism. I have other coping mechanisms, but nothing works as effectively as cutting, especially when I am at my peak of my anger.

In past sessions, I was under the impression that she understood my motivation to cut better than the average Joe, but now I don't think that's true. I think what scares her is my saying that I wouldn't take cutting out of my tool kit of coping mechanisms because of its effectiveness. Never once does she give me another coping mechanism. She just says that I have to stop. She also says that I have to learn how to sit with my anger. What the hell does she think I spend all my time doing anyway?

I have decided that I am never going back to her. She is moving out of the South Bay in two weeks anyway, so I shouldn't have a difficult time convincing my mom to let me stop.

When I get home, I find a direct Instagram message from a stranger in Peru. It reads, "fucking liar piece of shit." That further dampens my mood. Like, at least send me a string of curse words in Spanish, so I can build up my Spanish vocabulary. Maybe I should just delete my Instagram account. That's probably a good idea.

Los Angeles: Wednesday, April 17th, 2019

My mom is in Peru, and she is worried that she will be stuck in the hearing until three in the morning because Sandro Monteblanco said that sometimes trials like these can last that long. For some reason, the psychologist who interviewed me doesn't make an appearance, so the witnesses have to pause. The medical examiner validates our claims that a rape could have occurred, but because the psychologist didn't show up, my mom is unable to testify.

Now there is going to be a third hearing set for May 2nd. Thankfully, the judge tells my mom she doesn't have to be present for that. The next hearing is in a week, and my mom and psychologist should testify then.

I have been able to dive into the schoolwork I have to do, so my mind hasn't been too preoccupied with the case. I miss my mom, and I just want her to come home. I convince her to let me stop going to therapy.

Los Angeles: Saturday, April 20th, 2019

I spend most of the day studying for AP Spanish. Lola and Bryan go out on a date, and around four in the afternoon, Lola runs into my room asking if she has any visible hickies on her neck, and then she runs out. That sums up her date for me. I am being moody because I still have feelings for Bryan.

I go to James' to study for English and Spanish. We are productive for two hours. Then we eat at Good Stuff in Redondo Beach. James makes a goal for himself to try to memorize all the waiters' names. At first, I thought it would be awkward having dinner as friends alone with him, but I have a great time. I never realized he could talk so much because in a group setting, he doesn't talk as much. I feel like I am able to see a different side of him. We are becoming closer friends, which I need right now because I have no idea what will happen between Bryan and me.

Case-wise there are no new updates, but my mom's still in Peru and my parents are mad at each other, so they aren't talking to each other. That's also my fault. Oh, I forgot to mention, my dad decided to stay home because he couldn't stand traveling with my mom. Originally, they were going to go to Peru together.

I talk to Bryan until midnight. I tell him that I used to have a crush on him. It comes out because I am exhausted. My mouth runs away when I'm tired. I have to work on controlling it better. This is why I should sleep in order to avoid making rash decisions that I will regret in the future. At least we both can be honest and open with each other now.

Los Angeles: Sunday, April 21st, 2019

I spend a while watching *Game of Thrones*. I am trying to figure out my feelings because I had a great time with James last night and part of me wants to like him as more than friends, but I'm still caught up on Bryan. Liking James would allow me to prove to myself that I don't like Bryan in that way.

I talk to Lola for thirty minutes, and I tell her that I would never have any romantic feelings for Bryan, which is a lie, of course. I only tell her that because she explicitly asks me. What if Bryan tells Lola? I wouldn't be surprised if he already has. Lola is upset because she is trying to get Bryan to swear off alcohol for her, but that's not something she can control. As much as she wishes to control him, she can't. She claims she loves him, but whenever she tells him she loves him he won't say it back. She tells me she is going to stop telling Bryan she loves him.

I wonder what Bryan's true feelings for Lola are. I want to talk to him about it, but I would do so at the peril of hurting myself because I love both of them. Plus, they are so busy with each other that neither has much time for me, and that is like a punch to the gut. They are both two of my closest friends, and I feel like I have lost them both. Whatever. It's time for me to branch out again.

Los Angeles: Wednesday, April 24th, 2019
Today is my mom's last day of testimony. I am antsy throughout my classes, but when they end, I have the chance to talk to my mom for an hour. The testimony goes well, and she says most of Vicente's witnesses had conflicting statements. She feels pretty good about her statement though. The psychologist who interviewed me didn't show up again, but there is going to be another hearing on the Second of May. My mom has hired a private investigator to try to find her. It's kind of suspicious that she is off everyone's radar.

While I am talking to my mom on the phone, I am lying on the main lawn at my school. My gaze keeps drifting towards Elliott, who is on the other side of the lawn talking to some of his friends. God, why do I still care about him? It's like I just wonder how he's doing.

James and I are working on applications for the Sustainability Council next year, and I feel like I am annoying James by repeating a list of everything we have to do. We have a theater play, which we run three consecutive times.

I have realized now that since Bryan and Lola are dating, they are less likely to keep secrets from each other. I can't trust them with anything individually. My issue is that I tell Bryan a lot more about myself than I do Lola, and if Lola found out some of the things I have told him, I think she would feel hurt. Ever since I told Bryan that I used to like him, Bryan has been more cautious and won't spend any time alone with me. I have to move on and stop caring. I managed to basically lose that friendship, so screw it.

Los Angeles: Monday, April 29th, 2019

Lola spends an hour talking to me about potentially breaking up with Bryan because she still thinks there is no "spark" in their relationship. Hell, I wish I had such a normal problem like that, but instead I have to decide whether or not to continue the case. I want to quit it for my own sanity, but I also want to continue to help encourage other women in Peru to find their voices.

The judge wants to interview the toxicologist expert we had speak on Beto Ortiz's show, but that hearing won't be until June 21st. That's so far away. My therapist asks me, "Mackenzie, what do you think broke after the rape?" I don't know how to answer that question. I feel broken, not whole, but I can't place my finger on what feels off. I compartmentalize all my feelings about what happened, but that means the feelings are locked in a box and stored in a dark place in the back of my mind. I realize that at some point that box will crack open. That thought scares me. Some of my emotions are starting to come back. Some days I still feel numb, but more and more, I have been feeling angry at the littlest things. It's a struggle to control anger. At least if I'm sad, I can just sit down and cry, but the anger can cascade into unpredictable actions.

I realize that because I have spent so much time being numb, I haven't been able to address my emotions in regard to my relationship with Elliott. I wish I could be a robot devoid of human emotions; that would make life so much easier.

Los Angeles: Tuesday, April 30th, 2019

The highlight of my day is after the Sustainability Council meeting. When I am talking to James and the co-presidents of the council, our council's faculty advisor comes up to James and me and tells us that we have been chosen to be the next leaders of the Sustainability Council.

As soon as everyone leaves the room, James and I are so happy and thrilled that we start crying and laughing simultaneously. I did quite a bit of work for the Earth Gram event, which is a fundraiser where people pay to have a Sustainability Council member deliver an eco-themed pick-up line to another student during class. The Sustainability Council member would wear a costume, and they would read the pick-up line to the entire class. One of my favorite lines is, "Are you an endangered redwood tree? Because you're tall, strong, and I want to hug you."

I don't think I deserved to be chosen as president. It is a complete surprise. Then James asks if I think Elliott would get mad at the fact that I have been chosen over him. I don't respond. James says Elliott isn't handling the situation right with me. God, I just don't care anymore.

On a side note, I am excited to write my English essay because it's about gender roles and sexual assault, my two favorite topics to rant about. Somehow today has become a good day!

MAY

Los Angeles: Thursday, May 2nd, 2019

All in all, today is a good day. I have all work periods at school. I decide to sleep in until noon and go to school after all my classes are over to potentially talk to Elliott again.

Yesterday, I had a conversation with Elliott. He is finally starting to talk to me, and the conversation was enlightening. A lot had happened between us that I wasn't aware of, and I was glad to put some of my emotions out on the table. We ended the conversation with both of us concluding that we had more to discuss, so today I spend the remainder of my free periods looking for Elliott. He is busy. Instead, Bryan and I play Magic: The Gathering.

There is another case hearing today. Vicente was supposed to testify, but his testimony is pushed back even further because the court once again couldn't contact the psychologist. The next hearing is on June 21st. At today's hearing, the maid at the party testified, yet another person I didn't talk to or even see, but her testimony was thrown out.

I am stressed about next week because it's the final push of the year, and all my classes have tests. I am ready to finish this year in style.

Los Angeles: Saturday, May 4th, 2019

I babysit from four in the afternoon until midnight.

I am upset because Bryan has told me he would FaceTime me when he returned from his flight back from Sacramento around ten at night. Of course, he talks to Lola first, and he doesn't call me until 11:30. I wish he'd called me when we'd agreed to call, but somehow Lola takes priority. That upsets me. By the time he calls, both of us are too tired to have a real conversation. I struggle to keep the hurt out of my voice and being tired exacerbates my struggle. I worry that I am being rude.

At some point, I have to tell Lola that I used to like Bryan. I feel like I am losing him more and more every day. I get home at 12:30 in the morning, but I don't feel like sleeping. I stay up until two in the morning writing a song with guitar accompaniment about Bryan. I should build up new walls because my vulnerability with Bryan only manages to hurt me.

Los Angeles: Sunday, May 5th, 2019

Every time my mom has to tell me info related to the case, she gets somber and says, "Mackenzie, I have to talk to you about something." So, when she walks into my room and says that phrase, I think, *here we go again.*

My mom told my sister's friend's mother about Peru, and that mother told her thirteen-year-old daughter, who then started asking my sister about it. This is why I am so adamant about maintaining control over the narrative. Of course, my mother didn't tell me she was going to tell my sister's friend's mom. I feel I'm being selfish by trying to control the narrative to my story, but the story has a mind of its own.

Now, there is a fourth hearing date set for July 3rd because the judge wants to interview the cook who was at the party where I was raped. I feel like this trial is veering off in an unproductive direction.

Los Angeles: Wednesday, May 8th, 2019

I took the AP Spanish test yesterday. It was long and tedious. I was jumpy all day.

I applied for this leadership position called CSAB at my school, which is an acronym for the Community Service Advisory Board. Last year I applied, and I wasn't accepted, which was devastating. In hindsight, it turned out to be a blessing because of everything I have had to deal with this year. Elliott is one of the members of the board interviewing me, and that throws me off. Last year both of us applied, but he had applied not because he wanted to do service, but for college applications. I also believe that he applied partly because I was applying. This was when we liked each other. We worked on our applications together, but now that friendship has been obliterated.

I leave the room in tears, not because I think the interview went poorly, but because having Elliott interview me takes a lot out of me, and I am just done. I don't think I will be accepted, or maybe I am just being cynical.

At home I hang out with Lola, and she goes on and on about Bryan and their issues. It pains me to talk to her about him. I need to place a moratorium with Lola on conversations about Bryan. In order to continue this charade, I need to put my own feelings aside, which I am capable of doing. I've been doing it since February.

Los Angeles: Saturday, May 11th, 2019

Today is a growth day. I spend a lot of time with Bryan. I learn that because I used to like him, he thinks that talking with me about Lola is awkward, and he wants to stop doing so. A huge part of our friendship is built on him trusting me with his feelings for Lola, whatever they may be. I am used to being the person he vents to about her, as I have been in the past.

Later, when I am back at home, Lola, Bryan, and Camila come over. Lola attaches herself to Bryan. She is lying on top of him. Camila says that their PDA is making her uncomfortable, so I ask them to separate in order to focus on our group game; nevertheless, just a minute later Lola is back sitting on top of Bryan.

Camila leaves, and Bryan, Lola, and I go to my school to watch my brother's theater performance. The drive is hilarious because Lola is sitting on Bryan the whole time, and her mom is watching the two of them from the rear-view mirror. Poor Bryan. Despite him saying that her actions are embarrassing him, she doesn't stop. He has to get a handle on his girlfriend.

My brother's performance is amazing, and my entire family keeps complimenting him, but he keeps trying to refute the compliments.

When Bryan arrives back at his house, he FaceTimes me. NOT Lola, ME. I realize that regardless of how close he and Lola end up, Bryan will always want me as a friend.

Los Angeles: Sunday, May 12th, 2019

I babysit until nine at night, but I talk to Rafe's mom until midnight. For some reason, I open up to her and tell her about the hospitalization and my lack of trust in my mother. She opens up to me about the hard struggles she went through after her rape. She is a great sounding board, and I am able to share parts of myself that I normally don't open up about. She also gives great advice. Being that we are both survivors, she can provide me with support different from the majority of the other people in my life.

Los Angeles: Monday, May 13th, 2019

It has been ten months of absolute hell. The defense council submits some "new evidence," whatever that means, and Sandro Monteblanco isn't sure what that is yet. He knows that some of the evidence includes "legal expert opinions." He predicts that some of the evidence is going to be based on my original testimony and that the defense will try to claim that I didn't act like a rape victim while giving testimony. First off, how the hell are rape victims supposed to act? I am one, and I can't answer that question. The defense also files a motion requesting the dismissal of my mom's testimony, but that likely won't be passed by the judge. They also request that I be re-interviewed. I hope their requests aren't accepted.

Los Angeles: Wednesday, May 15th, 2019

When I get home from school my mom seems a little off. I try to talk to her, but she doesn't want to talk.

I go to Lola's, and around 8:45 at night my dad calls me telling me that I have to come home as soon as possible. I walk into my kitchen to find my mom yelling at my dad because she thinks he is trying to change family therapy to once every other week rather than our typical once a week. She proceeds to call him some hurtful names before collapsing to the floor, at which point my dad leaves the room. My sister tries to comfort my mom, and I feel uncomfortable leaving her alone to comfort my mom, so I stay in the kitchen. Then my mom yells at me and calls me weak because she claims I don't voluntarily talk about the rape. She is deflecting her internal pain and taking it out on my entire family. My mom thinks that I am suicidal, which isn't true. Not once, even during all this chaos, did I ever try to kill myself. My sister is so freaked out by the cascade of events that she convinces me to spend the night in her room.

Los Angeles: Thursday, May 16th, 2019

Yesterday, my mom lost her cool, and today the penance is loads of therapy. I go to a new therapist because my old one moved out of the South Bay. I have the pleasure of filling in my new therapist on the last nine months. I don't have the chance to talk about what's upsetting me because I am so busy filling her in.

Then my mom, dad and I go to the family therapist, and we spend the whole time talking about my mom. My mom's excuse for her flipping out on the family is that she drank a margarita, but I feel like she is blaming the alcohol for her emotions, which she should know how to control better. It's one thing to be upset, but it's another to redirect your upset feelings toward other people.

My parents manage to end up getting mad at each other, but my dad reminds everyone in the room that the reason he comes to therapy is to help my relationship with him not his relationship with my mother. I think he is making excuses to avoid dealing with the issues he has with my mom. I stay silent.

Skid Row: Friday, May 17th, 2019

Guess what I found out this morning? Elliott is doing twenty-four hours of homelessness. Twenty-four hours of homelessness is a period of twenty-four hours during which my school goes downtown to

Skid Row to volunteer at the Los Angeles mission. A year ago, Elliott and I were happily dating when we went to the event together, and now he can't even stand to look at me. Talk about serious tension.

Surprisingly, the twenty-four hours of homelessness goes better than I expect it to. We decorate poster boards and serve dinner to the homeless. Elliott and I are cordial, and we don't display any obvious tension. We talk a little, but all the Chadwick students hang out together.

Elliott doesn't have his phone, so he asks to borrow mine to send a text to his mom. Ironically, right as he is texting her, Bryan sends me a joke about Elliott and me, which isn't something I want Elliott to see, but I swear he does. Bryan is great at making ill-timed jokes. I wish I could turn back the clock and be friends with Elliott again. I also wish that someone could tell me what to do to fix this situation because I don't know how to.

Los Angeles: Sunday, May 19th, 2019

I feel very sleep deprived, so much so that I crave human attention. Yesterday, Bryan and Lola went on a date, and I know it isn't my business, but Lola keeps talking to me about it.

Camila and I eat lunch at Green Temple, but I am in a bad mood. Camila and I go shopping, but I don't feel like spending any money, so it is just window-shopping for me. Then as Camila is about to leave, I ask James if he wants to come get some frozen yogurt. After Camila leaves, I hang a little with James, but Bryan finds out, and he is upset that I didn't invite him.

Los Angeles: Friday, May 24th, 2019

The end of the year is so close. I can taste the freedom already. I have started having flashbacks of last year in Peru. This time the flashbacks take place prior to the rape. I miss the fun, jubilant Mackenzie.

After my classes end, Bryan and I go out to lunch because now he has his driver's license. We have Thai food. I understand that the reason I am upset with him and Lola being together is because it takes away time I could spend with him in a platonic way. I open up to him more about the cutting, but now I regret it. I still haven't told any of my other friends. On the drive to my house from the restaurant, Bryan drives behind me because he doesn't know the way. Every time we stop at a stop light, I look in my rearview mirror and I can see him singing to whatever song he is playing on his stereo. It cracks me up.

We meet up with our friends at my house. Once again, Lola spends quite a bit of time lying on top of Bryan, and it makes everyone in the room uncomfortable. At one point, James gets weirded out and leaves the room.

Bryan leaves at seven, which feels too early, and James leaves shortly after. Lola and I spend the rest of the time talking about Bryan. I call James around ten to check in with him, and we talk until midnight.

Los Angeles: Saturday, May 25th, 2019

I babysit from ten in the morning to ten at night for both Rafe and the girls. Taking care of kids is an excellent distraction from life.

Bryan calls me after Rafe has gone to bed. While we are talking, he tells me the reason he had to leave my house early last night was because his parents blame him for not doing more to smooth out the conflict between his cousin and me. Bryan has nothing to do with any of that. I invited Elliott over last night. It's not my fault or Bryan's that Elliott decided not to come. I listen to Bryan and try to give him support.

I call James because I still need someone to vent to about my issues. I can't burden Bryan with my issues because he is already upset. It turns out James is a good sounding board.

Los Angeles: Sunday, May 26th, 2019

My body isn't ready to roll out of bed this morning. I want to at least clean my room before leaving to hang with Bryan and James. I explain to Bryan that I am not comfortable inviting Lola to hang with us because the PDA between her and Bryan is grossing me out. I have asked her to stop, but she doesn't. He seems to understand, or at least I hope he does. We walk from James' house to King Harbor to get Mexican food.

On Friday, I made it clear to Bryan that he can never use me in any way to make Lola jealous because I refuse to be in the middle of their business. I love how I keep telling myself to stay out of Bryan's and Lola's business, but somehow, I always end up right back in the middle of it. I have to learn how to set better boundaries for myself.

On Saturday, when we were all hanging out, I had to tell Bryan to stop hugging me because I could tell Lola was getting upset. I get the feeling that, for some reason, I don't know why, he is trying to make Lola jealous. I don't know if he is doing it intentionally, but I had to set clear boundaries with him, nonetheless.

Now, Bryan wouldn't hug me. I have the chance to clarify that I appreciate his hugs as long as Lola isn't around.

I think James and I are becoming closer. His mom texted mine asking if James and I were dating, and my mom responded with, "I sure hope they will be." Of course, I told James. The thing is, even if James likes me, he would never do anything about it because of his loyalty to Elliott, so I don't have to worry. Plus, I still like Bryan.

When I get home, Lola asks to hang, which progresses to a sleepover. It is hard to explain to Lola what I did all day without mentioning that Bryan and I hung out. I feel guilty now, and I know I should come clean. Lola takes my favorite bra out of my closest without asking me and calls Bryan. I sit in another room, not realizing that she is "borrowing" my bra while I work on homework.

Los Angeles: Monday, May 27th, 2019

James said something interesting. He told me he thinks Elliott still has feelings for me, which would explain the hatred vibes. I still don't know what I did wrong.

My mom and I go out for coffee, and we start talking about Elliott. My mom says something that makes me cry. She tells me, "Mackenzie, you once told me that the reason you loved him was because of the person he was and that he accepted you for you." I have no clue why that makes me cry. It just does. My mom and I write a text to Bryan's mom to clarify that Bryan has nothing to do with my issues with Elliott. Surprisingly, she responds right away that she will talk to her son and nephew about it.

Lola is convinced that I like Elliott. It's better she thinks that than the truth. Somehow, despite all of Elliott's hatred towards me, I am not angry with him. Part of me wants to be angry with him and hate him because he abandoned me while I was going through utter hell, but I just can't. Unlike Bryan, Elliott wasn't there for me when I needed him most. I have a lot of emotions that I have to sort out. Thankfully, summer is coming.

Los Angeles: Friday, May 31st, 2019

It's the second to last Friday of the school year, and I am in a bad mood. I have nothing to do this weekend because I have been productive, and the last thing I want to do is spend quality time with my thoughts.

I have debate club with Bryan, which is a joke. In the beginning of the year, we used the telepresence room to FaceTime multiple schools on the East Coast, and we would have mock debates, but the members of the club at my school eventually stopped calling the other schools altogether. Then all the club members stopped showing up. Now, it's just Bryan and me sitting in a room every Friday, talking.

After school I babysit for the girls, and they decide to paint my nails and spray some hairspray in my hair. I receive a whole makeover. James and I decide to have lunch on Sunday together, so we can also edit our English essays, but we never decide on a time. He isn't responding to my texts. I feel like he's avoiding me.

JUNE (AGAIN)

Los Angeles: Saturday, June 1st, 2019

I spend the morning trying to be productive. Camila comes over, and we walk to the coffee shop. Camila is doing well, but I feel like she is pushing me away because this summer she is spending seven weeks at Harvard. I can't say I am surprised. But I'm not ready to let her go yet. I am looking forward to summer.

I text James again, but he doesn't respond for eight hours, and when he responds, he says *IDK* to my question about what time we should have lunch tomorrow. It's obvious now that he doesn't want to. Now, I have to cancel gracefully.

My mom and I watch *Rocketman,* which is a movie based on Elton John's life. It is spectacular. I recommend watching it.

When I return home, I obsessively sort Magic cards for five hours because I am stressed with the James stuff, which I don't want to let bug me at all. I thought we were becoming closer friends. Now that he has ghosted me, I'm not so sure.

Los Angeles: Sunday, June 2nd, 2019

James has been avoiding my texts. I text him, "I have to cancel because I am feeling under the weather." I decide to take a nap instead. I need it.

My mom is in a fierce battle with my sister. I feel like nowadays they are constantly fighting. I can't pick sides, so I end up being caught in the middle of various arguments.

Oh, and Bryan and Lola broke up. All I know is that Lola broke up with Bryan, but other than that I'm not sure what happened because neither will talk to me about it.

Los Angeles: Wednesday, June 5th, 2019

I have my last theater show. My group created this comedy skit, and during lunch, we perform it to who-ever wants to come and watch. I am done with thea-ter, which is sad because I won't take it next year. I want to double up on science classes instead.

After the skit I am sitting on the main lawn, and Bryan joins me. He is starting to feel slightly better about the breakup with Lola, and we talk like old times. James joins us, and it feels amazing to sit under a tree and just laugh. The weather is nice, too.

I play quite a bit of guitar at home, and I am working on this new song. I am happy about the breakup, and I think that Bryan knows it. Bryan calls me, and we talk for an hour. He seems a little lonely. I guess he would normally spend this time talking to Lola.

Bryan asks if I have the directions to the place where the Community Service Advisory Board meeting that I am going to on Friday will be held. Bryan isn't on the board, and he is asking on behalf of Elliott who is on the other end of the line. For some reason, Elliott can't ask me himself, which is kind of strange. I guess he is still not talking to me. Maybe he's scared of talking to me.

Los Angeles: Saturday, June 8th, 2019

I receive about nine texts from Lola saying that I can't date Bryan. I am offended because I've already promised her I wouldn't date him, and I never told her that I liked him. Why is she so overprotective all of the sudden anyway? By breaking up with him, she relinquished her rights.

I go to lunch with my grandpa, who lives in Long Beach. On the way home I have a minor fender-bender. The car in front of me stopped suddenly, and

I barely grazed the back of it. I give the lady my number, and she says she will call me after getting estimates. I would rather pay in cash than go through insurance. I am so embarrassed. I regret not getting the lady's contact info because now I am just waiting for a response. I am not sure what to do because it is out of my hands. The other car wasn't badly damaged, but the lady seemed a little sketchy. I hope she is honest and won't try to scam her way into making money. My rule of thumb is just not to trust people anyway.

My dad is upset about the accident, but he helps me glue back together my license plate.

Bryan calls at 10:30 at night and accuses me of liking him. I think it is solely because he isn't taking Lola's breakup well. Maybe it helps boost his morale to believe that I like him. I do like him, but I tell him I don't. Nothing can happen anyway.

Los Angeles: Sunday, June 9th, 2019

I stay home nearly the whole day and do everything possible not to be productive. I play guitar and watch some Netflix. I go out and get coffee with my mom.

I am trying to figure out if I like Bryan. I don't think I do; however, I don't know how to explain how jubilant I am because of Bryan and Lola's breakup. Am I selfish? Lola calls me, and she seems to be doing okay, but at around ten at night, I receive thirty-three texts from her describing how much emotional pain she is in because of being single. I hope she doesn't do anything drastic. Who am I kidding? This is Lola.

I am so hyped for summer. It needs to arrive a hell of a lot faster. I have made the conscious decision not to study for my math final. I have some free time, so I start reading a book. It is the first book I have read for fun in months. Two more days left until summer!

Los Angeles: Monday, June 10th, 2019
Despite not studying for math, I think the final goes well.

I go to therapy, and we talk about how I struggle to let people in. I can tell my therapist wants me to open up to her. I am hesitant because everyone else I open up to has let me down in some way or another. They don't understand or collapse around me like my mother. This therapist is my third individual therapist this year, and I have had three separate family therapists as well in a span of seven months.

As much I want to open up to my therapist, I am not ready to talk about the night of the rape. Every time I tell the story of the rape, I speak about it as if I'm talking to my lawyer or the Peruvian press, so my speech is formal. Even when I tell my friends, I speak about it formally. My therapist wants me to open my heart and delve into my feelings about that night. It's not happening.

I have coffee with my mom. I tell her she is lucky to have the ability to open up to people about the various hardships in her life, and I start crying. I realize that what happened to me is not something I can just talk about at random. It takes a lot out of me to tell my story, even the legal version. I want to forget about the rape, the case, and the betrayals, so I can pretend nothing happened. Everyone tells me forgetting about it isn't healthy. Well, screw them. They don't understand.

Lola asks Bryan to date her again. Bryan is thinking about it. My prediction is he is going to date her even though she repeatedly hurts him. She broke up with him the last time. I won't give him any advice because he won't take it anyway. Plus, I don't think he wants my advice right now. But if I were to give it to him, I would tell him to stay away from her because she will continue to hurt him.

Los Angeles: Tuesday, June 11th, 2019
The history discussion final goes well, or so I think. Then I come home and watch *The Office* for about an hour before driving to Starbucks to meet my theater class. During mid-terms and finals, my drama teacher always treats his students to Starbucks, and we all appreciate it. This is my second year of having

him, and he is just amazing. Even though he yelled at me in September, I still really admire him as a person.

I want to have some time to talk to Bryan; however, I don't get a chance to. Now that I am on summer break, I don't know what to do with myself. I am running on leftover adrenaline from stress. I will crash in the near future. Bryan and I barely talk; he is busy working on his history project because his group decided to wait until the last minute. I text Lola, and she hasn't heard from Bryan.

I write a song for my dad for Father's Day, and I hope he likes it.

Los Angeles: Wednesday, June 12th, 2019

I clean my room and buy ten books for ten dollars at a second-hand bookstore. I also have boba. I am trying to get Bryan to make plans for tomorrow, but he's being annoying about it. Camila and I make plans and we just invite Bryan.

I have coffee with my mom, and we talk about summer plans. She is convinced I should start studying for the SAT. I agree with her, and I will start studying in a couple of weeks.

Bryan and I talk for a while over FaceTime, and he is also done with his finals. My mom is worried that my siblings and I won't get along this summer vacation, and I agree with her. It might be a struggle to avoid fighting.

I am going to miss Peanut. I won't see him for the next three weeks while I'm out of town.

Los Angeles: Thursday, June 13th, 2019

I hang out with Camila, Bryan, and James. It is a bittersweet hangout because it's the last time we will hang out together for a while. I am going to miss them.

Bryan friend-zones Lola again. I'm pretty proud of him for doing that. I didn't think he would make that wise decision.

It has been eleven months since the rape, and I do feel better. I can't say I can forget about the past because part of it is always within me, and I carry it everywhere I go. Thankfully, I have loving people who care about me, who have helped me through the rough patches.

I don't regret telling my mom about the rape. Had I not told her, my life would have been immensely more complicated, and I am not sure I would have been able to live with it. I don't regret pressing charges. I think the case has been and continues to be a vital step in my healing process. I feel like I still have a ways to go. I don't think I'll ever be over it, but at least I'm happy for now. Life is too short to dwell on the pain. I'm surprised that I feel almost a hundred percent normal. I learned a lot this past year.

I think that one of most valuable lesson I learned is that everyone has problems, so you can't judge someone else's hardships in comparison to your own. Everyone will have to spend time and energy dealing with their hardships, and it's better to figure out silver linings and work through them. Now, I understand what my therapist meant when she explained I had to sit with my anger. If you don't process your emotions, you can't move on.

EPILOGUE

Writing this book, in tandem with my continuous journaling, has helped me process my emotions and has helped me heal in many ways. At some point, I want to rewrite my story in a novel format, but I am not there yet. I plan to graduate high school and head off to college, but for now I have to put away this chapter of my life so that I can move on. Even though the court case continues, it is no longer at the center of my life. The future shines ahead of me, and I need to be able to walk into it, away from the shadow of my past.

I have grown so much, and I am so thankful for my family. I have learned that maintaining a support system, especially within your family, is not only vital to the recovery process, but it's also beneficial for anyone. No one needs to go through life alone. I am extremely fortunate to have the support network I have. I wish that I had trusted my parents more throughout the process. All they wanted to do was protect me. My parents taught me how to be resilient and to stand up for what I believe in. It's infinitely more difficult to deal with a sexual assault, or any trauma for that matter, in silence. Survivors should talk about their experiences with people they trust. Sexual assault thrives in silence, and as a society we have to work to destigmatize it. We have a ways to go; nevertheless, change is kindled at a grass roots level beginning with educating people about sexual assault and its aftermath.

This book is called *Monumental Silver Linings* because I learned so much from the aftermath of the assault. Everything I took away from this experience is a silver lining. Had I not been through my experiences, I wouldn't have learned these vital lessons. I learned how to build a robust support system. I learned how to ask other people for help. I discovered numerous healthy coping mechanisms for dealing with stress and intense emotions that I will be able to utilize for the rest of my life. I learned that change is stimulated by speaking up, and one little voice can change a country. I found my voice. I was able to be a voice for people who couldn't speak up. I learned that you can't help other people unless you help yourself first. I grasped the importance of setting boundaries with friends. I gained an understanding of the value of setting goals. Throughout this process, my goals have been to increase awareness of sexual assault and to be a voice for survivors who can't speak up. I wouldn't have been able to accomplish what I have, if I hadn't set clear goals for myself. Even with my goals, I wouldn't have been able to attain them without my family's support. One of the largest silver linings of the recovery process was being able to write this book. Writing this book has been therapeutic. I have been able to find memories related to the rape and its aftermath that I still need to work through and process, and the writing process has helped me heal tremendously.

It has been over two years since the rape, and now we are in the middle of a global pandemic. Just like I did while dealing with the rape, I am constantly finding silver linings while living through the COVID-19 pandemic. If it weren't for the pandemic, I wouldn't have time to write and publish this book.

Overall, I am doing well. I have begun my college application process. I am working on publishing a second book that will focus on all the strategies I used and am using in my journey to recovery. I found that as I dealt with the PTSD and watched my family suffer around me, I had to develop a tool kit in order to survive. I want to share my strategies with other people. My second book will be a guidebook to recovering from a sexual assault. It will be titled *How to* ~~Survive~~ *Thrive after a Sexual Assault.* One important topic that I will expand upon in my second book is cutting. If you are using this unhealthy coping mechanism, listen to someone who has been there. Don't cut yourself. By hurting yourself, you are making your difficult experiences worse. Try to find healthy coping mechanisms. You can take advantage of Google, my blog, or my second book.

Over these couple years, I have lost and gained many friends. I am no longer friends with Lola, Elliott, or Bryan. It's for the best. None of them are bad people, but they were unable to provide the support I needed. I am still close to Camila and James. They have supported me 100%. I am so grateful to have them in my life.

My family is also closer than ever, and with the pandemic, we have been able to spend a great deal of time together. I know that many couples who deal with trauma don't survive the aftermath, but my parents did. They held my family together, and now we are stronger than ever. They did the best they could. As a family, we are constantly evolving, and I am fortunate that my whole family has come out on the other end of this intact.

The United States Embassy banned my rapist and his parents from ever entering the United States. Honestly, even if the case doesn't end in a conviction, not being able to enter the United States is a significant punishment. Apparently, Vicente and his family were visiting the United States for college touring. They got stopped at the border, and that's when they discovered that their visas had been denied.

Shortly before the pandemic, the superior prosecutor expressed that the judge should hand down the maximum conviction possible for a minor (despite being of age, my rapist maintained the right to be tried and sentenced as a minor), which is twelve months in a juvenile detention center. We are awaiting the judge's ruling. We were supposed to find out the verdict on March 19th, 2020. Two days before the appointed ruling, all of Peru shut down because of COVID-19. Even if the judge rules in our favor, Vicente's family will likely appeal and take the case to the second stage of the Peruvian Court System, in which a verdict is decided upon by a panel of three judges. Regardless of the verdict from the panel of judges, the case will likely go to the Supreme Court of Peru. That will be the ultimate ruling. Even though the case hasn't made it there yet, other sexual assault cases in Peru have cited my case. In one case, a sexual assault survivor who reported her assault three years after it happened cited my case because I hadn't reported my rape until over two weeks afterwards. I am continuing to make a difference in Peru, but the case isn't the main focus of my life anymore. To anyone who is reading this in Peru or anywhere in the world, if you have been assaulted, speak up and tell someone close to you. I did all of this for you. We have never met, but I know you're out there, and I want you to heal and have some peace. Find your silver lining.

ACKNOWLEDGMENTS

I can't express my gratitude enough for all of the wonderful people who have helped through my recovery and writing process. So many people have supported me in my various endeavors, and I am thankful for each and every one of them.

First, I would like to thank my mom, who faced every hurdle I faced right along with me. She is the centerpiece of my support system. I couldn't ask for a better mother. I'll forever be grateful to my dad, GPPB, for being calm in all the chaos. Many thanks to my parents for all their advice and their willingness to drop everything in their schedules to take me out for coffee to talk about life. I wouldn't be the person I am today without you both.

I extend my gratitude to my younger siblings. I

know that my rape affected the whole family. It made life difficult for you guys, but I am so grateful that you both backed me one hundred percent. Your support means the world to me.

I want to thank my friends, especially those named in my book. All of you have helped me grow as a person. I want to extend my gratitude to Camila and Bryan in particular. Camila, you have a heart of gold, and your friendship means the world to me. Bryan, thank you for all the emotional support you provided me. Even though we may have drifted apart, I will always appreciate everything you did to help me pick up the pieces of my shattered life.

A special thanks to Christie Gleeson for being my sexual assault mentor and helping me through my recovery process. I admire your strength and fortitude. You have greatly impacted my life.

Many thanks to the Chadwick community. I have attended Chadwick for twelve years, and I am so grateful for my many experiences. Chadwick has greatly shaped who I am today.

I want to thank the dean of students the year following my rape, for the countless times that she provided support when I had trigger/panic attacks. She would leave meetings in order to devote time to helping me feel better. I appreciate all the teachers whom I told about my rape for being extremely supportive as well.

Finally, I want to thank the United States Embassy in Peru and my lawyer, Sandro Monteblanco, for providing exceptional legal support. The case wouldn't be where it is today without you guys. Thanks for helping me change a country!

RESOURCES FOR SEXUAL ASSAULT SURVIVORS AND THEIR FAMILIES

NAESV

The National Alliance to End Sexual Violence focuses on legislation that supports survivors and prevents sexual violence. It was created by a coalition of statewide organizations, local rape crisis centers, and advocates. NAESV has helped accomplish anti-sexual violence work at a national level.

Visit: https://endsexualviolence.org

NSVRC

The National Sexual Violence Resource Center provides leadership in preventing and responding to sexual violence through collaboration, sharing and creating resources, and promoting research.

Visit: https://www.nsvrc.org

RAINN

RAINN (Rape, Abuse and Incest National Network) is the nation's largest anti-sexual violence organization. RAINN created and operates the National Sexual Assault Hotline (800-656-4673), in partnership with more than 1,000 local sexual assault service providers across the country. RAINN also carries out programs to prevent sexual violence, help survivors, and ensure that perpetrators are brought to justice.

Visit: https://www.rainn.org

ABOUT THE AUTHOR

Mackenzie Severns is eighteen years old. She lives with her parents and two siblings in Los Angeles, California. She is a senior at Chadwick school, which she has been attending since first grade. When Makenzie isn't vigorously writing, she loves to hang out with her friends or play guitar. Mackenzie aspires to someday be a veterinarian. She is often found in the company of her beloved cat, Felix, or playing fetch with her dog, Pepper.

You can visit Mackenzie at
https://www.mackenzieseverns-activist.com/

If you have been through a similar experience and need any resources or someone to talk to, please don't hesitate to get in touch using the 'Contact Me' form on Mackenzie's website.

Made in the USA
Middletown, DE
05 October 2020

21176804R00128